THE WAY
PEOPLE
LIVE

Life Among the Great Plains Indians

Titles in The Way People Live series include:

THE WAY PEOPLE LIVE

Life Among the Great Plains Indians

by Earle Rice Jr.

Lucent Books, P.O. Box 289011, San Diego, CA 92198-9011

Library of Congress Cataloging-in-Publication Data

Rice, Earle.
    Life among the Great Plains Indians / by Earle Rice, Jr.
        p.   cm. — (The way people live)
    Includes bibliographical references and index.
    Summary: Describes the everyday life of the Native Americans living on
the Great Plains before the coming of the Europeans, covering their
religion, social customs, government, and art.
    ISBN 1-56006-347-5   (alk. paper)
    1. Indians of North America—Great Plains—History—Juvenile
literature.   2. Indians of North America—Great Plains—Social life and
customs—Juvenile literature.   [1. Indians of North America—Great
Plains.]   I. Title.   II. Series.
E78.G73R53   1998
978'.00497—dc21   97-27149
                                                                                             CIP
                                                                                             AC

Contents

Discovering the Humanity in Us All

The Way People Live series focuses on pockets of human culture. Some of these are current cultures, like the Eskimos of the Arctic; others no longer exist, such as the Jewish ghetto in Warsaw during World War II. What many of these cultural pockets share, however, is the fact that they have been viewed before, but not completely understood.

To really understand any culture, it is necessary to strip the mind of the common notions we hold about groups of people. These stereotypes are the archenemies of learning. It does not even matter whether the stereotypes are positive or negative; they are confining and tight. Removing them is a challenge that's not easily met, as anyone who has ever tried it will admit. Ideas that do not fit into the templates we create are unwelcome visitors—ones we would prefer remain quietly in a corner or forgotten room.

The cowboy of the Old West is a good example of such confining roles. The cowboy was courageous, yet soft-spoken. His time (it is always a he, in our template) was spent alternatively saving a rancher's daughter from certain death on a runaway stagecoach, or shooting it out with rustlers. At times, of course, he was likely to get a little crazy in town after a trail drive, but for the most part, he was the epitome of inner strength. It is disconcerting to find out that the cowboy is human, even a bit childish. Can it really be true that cowboys would line up to help the cook on the trail drive grind coffee, just hoping he would give them a little stick of pep-

permint candy that came with the coffee shipment? The idea of tough cowboys vying with one another to help "Coosie" (as they called their cooks) for a bit of candy seems silly and out of place.

So is the vision of Eskimos playing video games and watching MTV, living in prefab housing in the Arctic. It just does not fit with what "Eskimo" means. We are far more comfortable with snow igloos and whale blubber, harpoons and kayaks.

Although the cultures dealt with in Lucent's The Way People Live series are often historically and socially well known, the emphasis is on the personal aspects of life. Groups of people, while unquestionably affected by their politics and their governmental structures, are more than those institutions. How do people in a particular time and place educate their children? What do they eat? And how do they build their houses? What kinds of work do they do? What kinds of games do they enjoy? The answers to these questions bring these cultures to life. People's lives are revealed in the particulars and only by knowing the particulars can we understand these cultures' will to survive and their moments of weakness and greatness.

This is not to say that understanding politics does not help to understand a culture. There is no question that the Warsaw ghetto, for example, was a culture that was brought about by the politics and social ideas of Adolf Hitler and the Third Reich. But the Jews who were crowded together in the ghetto cannot be understood by the Reich's politics. Their life was a day-to-day battle for existence, and the creativity and methods they used to prolong their lives is a vital story of human perseverance that would be denied by focusing only on the institutions of Hitler's Germany. Knowing that children as young as five or six outwitted Nazi guards on a daily basis, that Jewish policemen helped the Germans control the ghetto, that children attended secret schools in the ghetto and even earned diplomas—these are the things that reveal the fabric of life, that can inspire, intrigue, and amaze.

Books in The Way People Live series allow both the casual reader and the student to see humans as victims, heroes, and onlookers. And although humans act in ways that can fill us with feelings of sorrow and revulsion, it is important to remember that "hero," "predator," and "victim" are dangerous terms. Heaping undue pity or praise on people reduces them to objects, and strips them of their humanity.

Seeing the Jews of Warsaw only as victims is to deny their humanity. Seeing them only as they appear in surviving photos, staring at the camera with infinite sadness, is limiting, both to them and to those who want to understand them. To an object of pity, the only appropriate response becomes "Those poor creatures!" and that reduces both the quality of their struggle and the depth of their despair. No one is served by such two-dimensional views of people and their cultures.

With this in mind, The Way People Live series strives to flesh out the traditional, two-dimensional views of people in various cultures and historical circumstances. Using a wide variety of primary quotations—the words not only of the politicians and government leaders, but of the real people whose lives are being examined—each book in the series attempts to show an honest and complete picture of a culture removed from our own by time or space.

By examining cultures in this way, the reader will notice not only the glaring differences from his or her own culture, but also will be struck by the similarities. For indeed, people share common needs—warmth, good company, stability, and affirmation from others. Ultimately, seeing how people really live, or have lived can only enrich our understanding of ourselves.

The Plains and the People

"We are descended from the eagle. We are an eagle nation. That is good, something to be proud of, because the eagle is the wisest of birds. He is the Great Spirit's messenger; he is a great warrior. That is why we always wore the eagle's plume, and still wear it. We are a great nation. It is I, Lame Deer, who said this."[1]

And just as the eagle flies high and soars freely across the wide expanses of the sky, so too did the Sioux once roam the Great Plains from horizon to horizon. Unfettered as their high-flying forebears, they followed the sun and the stars and the migratory paths of the buffalo. Life on the plains—for the Sioux and for all other Plains Indians—was hard but good.

The Great Plains

The Great Plains begin at the central lowlands in the east and continue westward about five hundred miles to the foot of the Rocky Mountains. Framed in the north by isolated mountains—the Black Hills, Judith Mountains, Bearpaw Mountains, Sweetgrass Hills, and others—the plains extend southward deep into central Texas, where they play out at the Rio Grande.

Geologists define the land as semiarid. Rainfall averages less than twenty inches annually on the plains; runoff routinely measures less than an inch a year, an amount insufficient to form free-flowing streams. The relatively high rainfall watersheds in the towering Rockies, however, form streams that add their slaking moisture to the land's parched, alkaline subsoil. Some of these mountain streams widen in their eastward flow and mature into swift-flowing rivers.

The 2,700-mile-long Missouri River, with its tributaries—the Bighorn, the Yellowstone, the Arkansas, and the Platte—drains the northern and central plains. The 1,450-mile-long Arkansas River, with its tributaries—the Red River, the White River, the Washita, and several lesser rivers—provides drainage for the southern plains. Both the Missouri and Arkansas River complexes form a part of the great Mississippi River system.

Moving westward from the Mississippi, the land stretches out in a vast expanse of windswept grasslands called prairies. This "sea of grass," as it was once called, extends to about the middle of the "prairie" states—the Dakotas, Nebraska, Kansas, and a portion of northeastern Texas.[2] The long-rooted grasses often grew as tall as ten feet on the prairies, until the irresistible advance of civilization claimed much of the land for farms, roads, cities, and towns.

From the western edge of the prairies, the grasses—mostly grama grass—become short with shallow roots, as the land slopes gently and steadily upward to form the more barren plateau, or steppes, of the Great Plains. Willow and cottonwood trees favor the meandering riverbanks in the lower regions of the plains, but the uplands are mostly void of trees and subject to high winds. Plains dwellers traditionally erect windbreaks to protect themselves from howling icy winds during routinely frigid winters and irritating hot breezes in the invariably sweltering summers.

Tribes of the Plains

Archaeologists, anthropologists, historians, and other scholars still cannot establish the origins of Indian tribes on the Great Plains with precision and absolute certainty. Most experts in the field presently theorize that the Indians migrated across the Bering Strait to Alaska about forty thousand years ago, and thence into the Americas. Yet other authorities on ethnic origins think that some tribes have always inhabited all parts of North America, while allowing that others may have migrated across the strait or navigated both the Atlantic and Pacific Oceans in sea vessels of some sort. Many Indians support the premise that some tribes were always on the plains, among them the Apache, Blackfeet, Arapaho, Kiowa, and Sioux. For example, Vine Deloria Jr., a writer and member of a prominent Lakota (Western Sioux) family, refutes the Bering Strait theory:

There are no well-worn paths which clearly show migratory patterns from

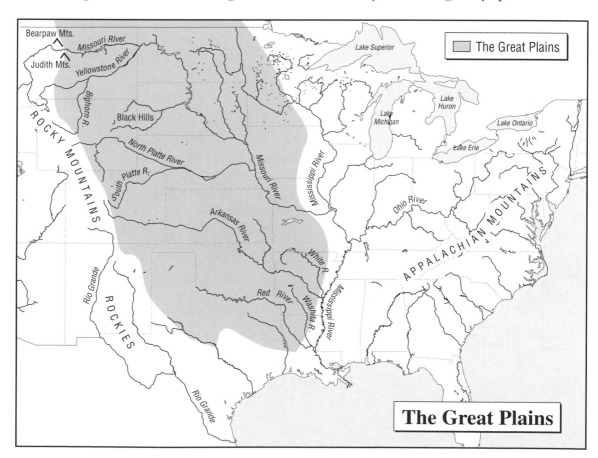

The Great Plains

Asia to North America, and if there were such paths, there would be no indication anywhere which way the footsteps were heading. We can be certain of only one thing: the Bering Strait theory is preferred by whites and consequently becomes accepted as scientific fact.[3]

The popular Kiowa author N. Scott Momaday agrees:

> I am an American Indian, and I believe that I can therefore speak to the question of America before Columbus with a certain advantage of ancestral experience, a cultural continuity that reaches far back in time. My forebears have been in North America for many thousands of years. In my blood I have a real sense of that occupation.[4]

Historian Thomas E. Mails also concurs. "The Blackfeet were in MacKenzie River country by 500 B.C. and Coronado found Apaches in present-day Texas in A.D. 1541," he writes. "The other tribes migrated to the Plains from the east or west as intertribal pressures and the lure of buffalo encouraged them." Mails further notes that the more powerful Eastern Woodland tribes forced the westward migration of weaker tribes, with each tribe emerging on the plains under pressure from the next emerging tribe to move farther and farther west:

> Thus about 1700 A.D. the Sioux moved from the Woodlands to Minnesota, and then to the Black Hills—forcing the Crows and Cheyennes on just ahead of them. Once horses were obtained, each migrant tribe began to stand its own

A village of the Mandan tribe. Scholars maintain that Indians migrated to North America from Asia, but others believe that certain tribes have always inhabited the plains.

ground, and although contested, well-boundaried tribal areas were established. Soon, even the great Woodland tribes decided it was best to leave them alone.

From approximately 1775 on most of the shifting ceased, the various Plains domains were set, and because of the spread of the horse, a common buffalo-and-horse-oriented pattern of life had emerged which lasted until about 1875, the end date varying somewhat according to what happened to each tribe in its contact with the Whites.[5]

The Plains tribes peaked in population at about the turn of the nineteenth century. All together they numbered about 200,000 people. As might be expected, the dominant tribes on the plains were those largest in number: the Blackfeet (30,000) and Assiniboin (10,000) tribes on the northern plains; the Sioux (27,000) and Pawnee (10,000) tribes on the north-central and central plains, respectively; and the Comanche (10,000) and Osage (6,200) tribes on the southern plains.

Root Languages and Tribal Origins

To better grasp and more easily study the relationships of these tribal groups, anthropologists and ethnologists classified them according to their spoken languages. Although differences of intertribal dialects posed some problems, members of the same language family could communicate verbally with one another, sometimes offsetting their differences by the use of a highly developed sign language. But communications between members of different language families was accomplished almost entirely by sign language. Occasionally, however, a few members of one family would learn the language of two or three other families to aid in intertribal talks over trade, boundaries, or alliances.

The Advent of the Horse

Neither similarity of language nor belonging to the same language family guaranteed harmony among the tribes of any given grouping. By and large, peace prevailed among the Plains tribes until the introduction of the horse by the Spaniards in the mid-1500s. Thereafter, pleasant intertribal relationships

Plains Indians relocate their camp. The majority of Plains tribes migrated according to the movement of the buffalo herds.

faded in a rush to acquire and dominate new homelands, as historian Richard White points out:

> By the nineteenth century, mounted [Indian] horsemen dominated vast sections of the trans-Mississippi West. As they acquired the horse, they often changed their homelands, making the plains and prairies and desert lands of the Southwest a seething cauldron of peoples. The Comanches, Utes, Arapahos, Cheyennes, Crows, Sioux, Osages, Kiowas, and numerous other peoples changed their lives and their locations during the tumultuous eighteenth century.

> Two groups in particular, the Comanches on the southern Plains and the Sioux on the northern Plains, signified the rising dominance of the nomads. The

Comanches, advancing out of southwestern Wyoming, in alliance with the Utes, pushed the Plains Apaches from their rancherias [camps]. They attacked the Navajos, raiding their herds and pushing them farther west to what is now the Navajos' home. . . . The Comanches raided both the New Mexican settlements and the string of missions that the Spanish established in Texas. . . .

> When epidemics in the 1770s weakened the powerful horticultural villagers of the Missouri—the Mandans, Arikaras, and Hidatsas—the Sioux seized the advantage and spilled out on the Plains, leaving the villagers surrounded by nomads who raided or traded as conditions permitted. . . . By the early nineteenth century a loose alliance among the Sioux, the Arapahos, and the

Cheyennes dominated the northern Plains. They faced significant challenges only from the Blackfeet who were moving south from Canada and the still strong Pawnees of the central Plains.[6]

While the advent of the horse may not have initiated intertribal hostilities, the increased mobility that it brought to the Plains Indians enabled them to strike farther, faster, and harder against rival tribes—and later against the white intruders who sought to divest them of their land and lifestyle.

Disunity and Vulnerability

Because conflicts contributed greatly to the daily life of the Plains Indians—from small, intertribal skirmishes to large-scale encounters with the U.S. Army—students of the era invariably want to know which tribes produced the finest warriors. Although any such judgment is necessarily subjective, the Blackfoot tribes of the northern plains appear to have been most feared by rival Indians and whites alike. The Lakotas ran a close second across the central plains. Warriors like Oglala chief Red Cloud epitomized their fighting spirit.

In 1866, upon learning of the government's plan to build forts along the Bozeman Trail that stretched from Julesburg, Colorado, to the Montana gold fields, Red Cloud stormed out of a peace council at Fort Laramie, Wyoming. He left white negotiators with these words: "Why do you pretend to negotiate for land you intend to take by force? I say you can force us only to fight for the land the Great Spirit has given us."[7] His action marked the beginning of Red Cloud's War, in which he and his band effectively shut down the Bozeman Trail.

The dominant Comanche, guided by such resolute leaders as Quanah Parker, earned the reputation as the most fearsome fighters on the southern plains. When he and his band of Kwahadi Comanche refused to attend peace talks at Medicine Lodge Creek, Kansas, in 1867, Quanah sent a message to white officials: "My band is not going to live on the reservation. Tell the white chiefs that Kwahadies are warriors."[8] Quanah and his band spent the ensuing eight years raiding the Texas plains, virtually without defeat.

The Blackfoot confederation, Lakota, and Comanche owed part of their notoriety to their superior numbers, but size alone did not always dictate the outcome of battle. Much of the fighting occurred between small war or raiding parties and thus emphasized individual fighting prowess. Some of the smaller tribes noted for their skills and

Red Cloud, the Oglala chief who fought the U.S. government for control of the Bozeman Trail.

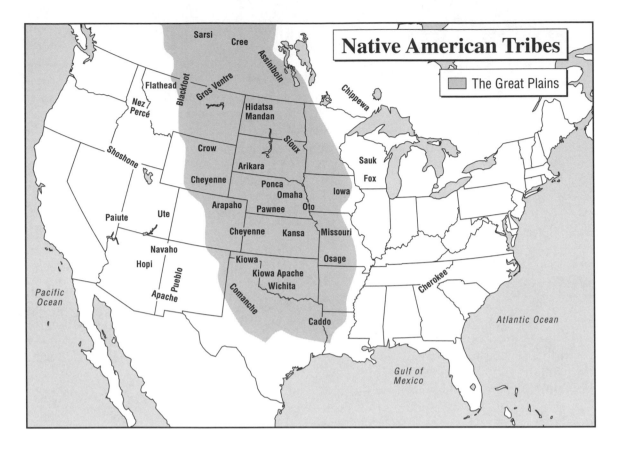

Native American Tribes

The Great Plains

Sarsi
Cree
Assiniboin
Flathead
Nez Percé
Gros Ventre
Blackfoot
Chippewa
Hidatsa
Mandan
Sioux
Shoshone
Crow
Arikara
Sauk
Fox
Cheyenne
Ponca
Omaha
Iowa
Arapaho
Pawnee
Oto
Paiute
Ute
Cheyenne
Kansa
Missouri
Navaho
Osage
Hopi
Kiowa
Pueblo
Kiowa Apache
Wichita
Apache
Comanche
Caddo
Cherokee

Pacific Ocean

Atlantic Ocean

Gulf of Mexico

ferocity in battle included the Cheyenne, Arapaho, Crow, and Shoshone. The least aggressive of the Plains tribes were the stationary village dwellers, who fought mostly in self-defense.

In the end, however, despite their formidable fighting qualities, the failure of the Plains Indians to turn aside intertribal rivalries and unite in a common cause laid them bare to white expansionism.

The Best Years

Except during the worst winter months, most of the Plains Indians followed the buffalo.

Their survival depended on their skills as hunters, first on foot and later on horseback. Even the stationary village tribes hunted on occasion to supplement their mostly vegetarian diets or to see them through seasons of poor or failed crops. Neither lifestyle was either able or destined to withstand the advance of white-styled civilization.

The best years of the Plains Indians' culture spanned little more than a hundred years, commencing about the same time as the birth of the United States. Sadly, but inevitably, life as they knew it during those golden years ended forever on December 29, 1890, beside a narrow creek in South Dakota called Wounded Knee.

Daily Life on the Plains: Dwellings

> "Everything an Indian does is in a circle, and that is because the power of the world always works in circles and everything tries to be round."
> —Black Elk, *Black Elk Speaks*

Life among the Indians of the Great Plains took two basic forms: the nomadic lifestyle of the buffalo hunters and the more permanent living mode of the farming tribes. The hunters lived almost exclusively on the higher elevations, where the buffalo roamed in vast numbers. "Once we were happy in our own country and we were seldom hungry," spoke Oglala holy man Black Elk, "for then the two-leggeds and the four-leggeds lived together like relatives, and there was plenty for them and for us."[9]

Farmers and Hunters

The farmers, such as the Osage, generally chose to dwell in the more fertile prairie lands. "The Osages are usually characterized by social scientists as fringe Plains Indians because they ventured onto the Great Plains for extended buffalo hunts twice yearly,"[10] writes Terry P. Wilson, a Potawatomi and professor emeritus of Native American studies at the University of California, Berkeley. Such annual tribal hunts were held in the spring or summer when migrating buffalo herds grazed close to the territory of agrarian tribes.

The principal hunting tribes inhabiting the plains during the 1800s were the Arapaho, Assiniboin, Blackfoot, Cheyenne, Comanche, Crow, Kiowa, and Sioux. Their agrarian, mainly prairie-land counterparts consisted of the Arikara, Kansa, Mandan, Osage, Pawnee, and Wichita.

Although Indians of both groups often shared commonalities of languages, customs, and cultures, their adopted lifestyles also accounted for pronounced differences in their daily lives. For example, the hunting tribes, finding it impractical to move swiftly about the plains in large tribal groups, routinely split themselves into bands, clans, or gentes (singular, gens)—tribal units common to both hunting and farming tribes—to pursue buffalo and other quarry. A band was made up of unrelated families, while a clan or gens consisted of families related by blood or marriage. Clan or gens members descended from the same ancestor; clan members shared the mother's lineage; members of a gens, the father's. Less encumbered in such bands, they would roam independently within specified boundaries, usually reuniting for a grand tribal buffalo hunt in the spring or fall, or both, and for the annual tribal games and Sun Dance in the summer.

"This ceremony, common to all Plains tribes, took place during the Moon of Making Fat (June) or the Moon of Blackening Cherries (July), always during the full moon, for it lit up the ignorance of the black sky," writes Blackfoot–Gros Ventre author James Welch. "The Lakotas called the ceremony *wiwanyag*

This Comanche tipi is a typical dwelling of the hunting tribes. The easily transported tipis were both comfortable and practical.

wachipi, or dance looking at the sun. Today it is called the Sun Dance."[11]

More rarely, the hunting tribes would band together in self-defense against hostile external forces. Conversely, the agrarian tribes maintained tribal solidarity in a stationary setting most of the time, frequently fortifying their villages behind earthen ramparts or stockades made of wood poles.

The Indian Tipi

For obvious reasons, Indians of the Great Plains used two types of dwellings: the renowned, highly mobile buffalo-hide tipi (also spelled *tipee*, *tepee*, or *teepee*) of the hunting tribes; and the lesser-known, more permanent earth or bark lodge used by the agricultural tribes. Even the more stationary tribes used the tipi while on the move.

Few dwellings can match the tipi for utility, mobility, and comfort. The word *tipi* comes from the Siouan language and means "used to dwell." Reginald and Gladys Laubin, recognized authorities on the tipi, write of it with admiration and affection:

No dwelling in all the world stirs the imagination like the tipi of the Plains Indians. It is without doubt one of the most picturesque of all shelters and one of the most practical movable shelters ever invented. Comfortable, roomy, and well ventilated, it was ideal for the roving life these people led in following the buffalo herds up and down the country. It also proved to be just as ideal in a more permanent camp during the long winters on the prairies. . . . Warm in winter, cool in summer, easy to pitch, and, because of its conical shape, able to withstand terrific winds or driving rain, the tipi is a shelter that should appeal to every outdoorsman. It is not only an all-weather tent but a home as well.[12]

The Plains tribes used tipis employing one of two possible pole arrangements: the three-pole base and the four-pole base, varying in construction from north to south. Historian and researcher of American Indian lore Frederick E. Hoxie notes:

In the north, among the Crows, Nez Perces, Crees, Blackfeet, Mandans, Arikaras, and Hidatsas, a four-pole base was common. These four central poles (usually made from pine saplings) were fastened together and partially buried in the ground. Several additional poles were arranged around them. Four-pole tipis are generally larger than the three-pole frames common to southern tribes such as the Shoshones, Cheyennes, Pawnees, Sioux, Kiowas, Kiowa Apaches, and Arapahos.

The traditional tipi covering was of bison hides carefully prepared and sewn together with sinew by the women of the tribe. . . . Smoke was ventilated through the roof of the tipi and could be directed with flaps that were opened and closed by poles outside of the covering. Doorways consisted either of holes cut into the hide covering and flapped open, or of triangular slits held in place by thongs. The bottom of the tipi was secured either by stakes or rocks, and the central pole

frame was anchored to the ground by a rope tied to a stake in the earth. A three-foot-high liner of separate material was typically lashed to the poles inside the tipi to provide insulation and protection against seepage or dew.[13]

In most tribes, although the man claimed ownership of the tipi, it really belonged to the woman. The woman made it, set it up, maintained it, and took it down. Every few days, while following the buffalo, she hauled it by horse- or dog-drawn travois ten or fifteen miles to a new campsite. (A travois is a crude vehicle consisting of two trailing lodge poles with a platform or net for carrying loads.) Such frequent moves left waste disposal to the elements and virtually eliminated sanitation problems. As a case in point, historian T. R. Fehrenbach notes that the Comanche "threw bones and scraps of food about, and littered the surroundings of their tipis. When the camp smelled too much, they moved."[14]

The Indian Lodge

The most common dwelling used by the Mandan and other farming tribes was the earth lodge, built from heavy cottonwood timbers, wickerwork, and sod. In 1833–1834, Prince Maximilian zu Wied, the German explorer and naturalist, together with Karl Bodmer, his Swiss-born artist companion, followed the Missouri River for some five thousand miles, during a year-long sojourn with the Plains Indians. On December 3, 1833, Maximilian spent the night in a Mandan earth lodge and recorded the following information in his journal, as noted by the editors of *People of the First Man*:

The entrance at the front of the hut could be closed by a door made of a piece of leather stretched on a frame and positioned directly behind the entrance. Behind this obstacle was a long, high, transverse wall made of woven willow rods and draped with hides as a protection against drafts. A lower wall, only three feet high, partitioned off the right portion of the hut as a stable for horses. The central fire pit was surrounded by the four main posts of the hut and four oblong benches made of basketry and covered with skins. Against the back wall was positioned a bed which Maximilian described as "consisting of a large square case made of parchment or skins, with a square entrance. They are large enough to hold several persons who lie very comfortably and warm on skins and blankets." [15]

This painting depicts the inside of a tipi. Smoke escaped through a hole in the top of the tipi, and a liner kept the interior warm and dry.

The grass lodge shown here was used by the Wichita; other types of lodges included animal-skin, wood, and sod.

Not all lodges were made from sod. Architectural structures on the prairies and plains were, of course, influenced by availability of building materials and tribal preferences. Author Elaine Andrews cites a pair of examples:

The Osage people of Arkansas and Missouri constructed oval or rectangular lodges made of mats or skins supported by a wooden framework. An Osage lodge could be as long as 30 to 100 feet and as wide as 15 feet. The Wichita people of Kansas used grass lodges. A series of poles arranged in a circle in the ground and bent together at the top formed the framework. Other poles were attached horizontally around this foundation, which was then covered with thick grass. The Wichita homes have been described as looking like giant beehives.[16]

An Indian dwelling was customarily positioned with its entrance facing east so that its occupants would be greeted each morning by the rising sun, a feature common to both tipis and lodges.

Sweat Lodges

In Walking in the Sacred Manner, *authors Mark St. Pierre and Tilda Long Soldier describe how an* Ini kagapi, *or sweat lodge, is used and for what purpose.*

"Water is placed on hot rocks; thus . . . the power of Iyan (the rock, the first physical being) is released in the form of steam, or *Taku S'kan s'kan* (the original energy in all things), taking the faithful back to the beginning of time.

In the sweat lodge, as in all Lakota ceremonies, the wisdom and help of the four directions—winds—are called upon by name for help and wisdom. *Mi' takuye' Oya' s'in* [literally, 'I acknowledge everything in the universe as my relations'] is uttered at various times during the sweat, reinforcing the idea that through the mysterious act of creation all things in the world are permanently related, as is a human family.

It is said that the sweat lodge itself is formed in the shape of ribs (Mother Earth's), and when the faithful emerge they do so as spiritually renewed people. . . . [T]he health of the *wana' gi*, the everlasting, intelligent soul—the permanent part of the human—is the principal concern."

The dome-shaped structure of the sweat lodge was said to represent the ribs of Mother Earth.

The nature, positioning, and arrangement of Indian villages or encampments, like dwellings, varied from tribe to tribe among both the hunting and farming communities.

Several factors influenced the selection of a site for a plains encampment. A good source of water for drinking, cooking, and bathing was essential. An ample supply of wood for fires was another prime consideration, as was adequate grazing land for horses to forage.

Villages and Encampments

The safety of band or clan/gens members and their horses constituted a camp leader's greatest responsibility. Thus, in choosing a campsite, an experienced camp leader—usually the band or clan/gens leader—looked for terrain features offering shelter from the elements and protection from intruders. Wherever possible, he would select flat, wooded lowlands buffered by ridges or bluffs to best provide safe haven for his charges. But at tribal gatherings, Plains Indians typically pitched their tipis on higher ground in a great circle. Bruce Grant, an author specializing in Indian and western lore, writes that their camps were

> usually located on or near the hunting grounds. To the unpracticed eye an Indian camp would look as if each family had

pitched its lodge or erected its dwelling where it fancied, but in reality such camps were carefully laid out.

Plains tribes on an annual hunt camped in a circle which was a quarter of a mile or so in diameter. Sometimes there were circles within circles. Each circle represented a family or political group. The Dakota [Eastern Sioux], who called themselves the "Seven Council Fires," formed their camps in two groups, one composed of four circles and the other of three.

The Omaha camped in a wide circle, with each of the ten families in its accustomed place. When the Kiowa, Cheyenne, and others held their annual sun dance or other ceremonies, they camped in a larger circle than usual, with each political division in a fixed and regular order.[17]

Although the village plan usually reflected family relationships, most tribes did not

A Comanche camp as portrayed by artist George Catlin. The locations and organizations of camps varied by tribe, but all groups sought safe sites with adequate water, firewood, and grazing land.

compel relatives to live in close proximity to one another. Freedom of choice generally ruled in such matters.

Along the upper Missouri River, the agrarian Mandan and Hidatsa oriented their villages around plazas that contained a barrel-shaped shrine to Lone Man, a culture hero believed to have initiated most of their tribal institutions. After visiting a Mandan village during the 1830s, artist George Catlin described its defensive characteristics:

> The ground on which the Mandan village is at present built, was admirably selected for defense; being on a bank forty or fifty feet above the bed of the river. The greater part of this bank is nearly perpendicular, and of solid rock. The river, suddenly changing its course to a right-angle, protects two sides of the village, which is built upon this promontory or angle; they have therefore but one side to protect, which is effectually done by a strong piquet [picket]. The piquet is composed of timbers of a foot or more in diameter, and eighteen feet high, set firmly in the ground at sufficient distances from each other to admit of guns and other missiles to be fired between them. The ditch (unlike that of civilized modes of fortification) is inside of the piquet, in which their warriors screen their bodies from the view and weapons of their enemies, whilst they are reloading and discharging their weapons through the piquets.

> The Mandans are undoubtedly secure in their villages, from the attacks of any Indian nation, and have nothing to fear,

Mandan villages were often located atop steep river banks for protection. The village's inland perimeter, not visible in this illustration, was secured with a picket.

The Sacred Circle

To the Plains Indians the circle symbolized the all-encompassing, never-ending connectivity of everything in the universe. In The Indians of the Great Plains, *Norman Bancroft-Hunt calls on the writings of Tyon, a mixed-blood Oglala, to explain the concept of the Sacred Circle. Writes Tyon:*

"The [Oglala] believe the circle to be sacred because the Great Spirit caused everything in nature to be round except stone. Stone is the implement of destruction. The sun and the sky, the earth and the moon are round like a shield, though the sky is deep like a bowl. Everything that breathes is round like the body of a man. Everything that grows from the ground is round like the stem of a tree. Since the Great Spirit has caused everything to be round mankind should look upon the circle as sacred for it is the symbol of all things in nature except stone. It is also the symbol of the circle that marks the edge of the world and therefore of the four winds that travel there. Consequently it is also the symbol of a year. The day, the night, and the moon go in a circle above the sky. Therefore the circle is a symbol of these divisions of time and hence the symbol of time.

For these reasons the [Oglala] make their tipis circular, their camp circle circular, and sit in circles in ceremonies. The circle is also the symbol of the tipi and of shelter. If one makes a circle for an ornament and it is not divided in any way, it should be understood as the symbol of the world and of time."

---

except when they meet their enemy on the prairie.[18]

Relative to the temporary encampments of the nomadic tribes, the more permanent villages of the farming tribes were usually strategically located on well-fortified, highly defensible sites.

Owing to their transitory nature, Plains-style campsites lacked elaborate fortifications and were often necessarily established in less than strategic locales.

Interestingly, according to Thomas E. Mails, a camp's location revealed something of its occupants:

A camp near water and away from all timber was probably Sioux, who had a deep respect for ambush; a camp on open prairie, but near timber, would be Cheyenne or Arapaho; a camp situated among open timber, Kiowa or Comanche; while smoke issuing from the cover of a dense thicket would indicate Osages, Omahas, or Pawnees.[19]

Apart from locational differences, however, Indian camps invariably held to a circular arrangement. "Without the circle there is no life," writes Cheyenne-Arapaho author John Redtail Freesoul. "Our forefathers perceived that if the circle of the nation's hoop was broken, then the buffalo would disappear, the land would be taken, and warriors would lose power."[20]

And while the nation's hoop remained unbroken, life was good for the people of the Great Plains.

CHAPTER 2

Daily Life on the Plains: Families and Functions

"The Indian was a providing family man, a protective mother, a teaching grandparent, a child learning to survive in a changing world."

—James Welch, *Killing Custer*

In the culture of the Plains Indian, the man was the hunter and the warrior, responsible for supplying meat and protecting the family; the woman took charge of the household and moving camp.

The Roles of Men and Women

The Indian woman, contrary to how she has been traditionally portrayed in movies and pulp fiction, did not play the fawning subordinate to the man of the family. Her position was respected, her labors appreciated, and her crafts valued. But generally her lot was not an easy one, as Maximilian observed:

The women, who in general are well-treated among the Blackfeet, have to perform all the heavy work. They pitch the tents, chop sod, and lay it around the hem of tents at the base. They cook, cut, gather and carry home the firewood, tan the hides, and care for the pieces of clothing. In short, they are rather busy.[21]

Nor was life easier for Wichita women, who "dominated village life" but "performed the majority of domestic chores."[22] Still, in the majority of Plains cultures, males honored the role played by females. For example, Mark St. Pierre and Tilda Long Soldier, his Oglala Lakota spouse, comment:

In Lakota society, the spiritual and economic powers of women were not only acknowledged but well respected. When a man took a wife, he lived in her camp. When the Lakota traced their ancestry, while acknowledging and respecting their father's relatives, most took the band name of their mothers. These patterns still exist.[23]

While it might seem that the men assigned the harder, less desirable tasks to the women, they did so for good reason. The men had to remain armed and ready to defend against enemy raiding parties that might strike at any time, usually attempting to steal their highly prized horses. When the village men mounted hunting or raiding parties, some always stayed behind to protect the camp. Tribes usually hunted within established tribal boundaries but occasionally strayed beyond their own territories, often resulting in lively confrontations with unappreciative neighbors.

In camp the women busied themselves for hours on end scraping and curing buffalo hides and using them to make bedding, robes, clothing, rawhide utensils, carrying cases (parfleches), and tipi covers. Little of the buffalo was wasted. Horns were fash-

Buffalo meat hangs on drying racks in this 1870 photo of an Arapaho camp in Kansas. Indian women were responsible for preparing food as well as fashioning buffalo hides into clothing and household items.

ioned into spoons and ladles. Even the hooves were cooked to yield glue. Other female duties included collecting all kinds of herbs, roots, berries, and usable plants and shrubbery, fetching the firewood, fixing the meals, and rearing the children.

The men spent much of their time in camp fashioning and repairing weapons for the hunt and hostile forays. Taking part in tribal government, village affairs, and camp security, playing games, and training boys to become hunters and warriors kept the men fully occupied.

Children of the Plains

Aside from providing meat and protection for the tribe, perhaps no male responsibility was more critical than instructing boys in becoming providers and protectors, especially the

latter. George Bird Grinnell, the famed naturalist and student of Indian life, wrote of the Cheyenne:

> The fighting spirit was encouraged. In no way could a young man gain so much credit as by the exhibition of courage. Boys and youths were trained to feel that the most important thing in life was to be brave; that death was not a thing to be avoided; that, in fact, it was better for a man to be killed while in his full vigor rather than to wait until his prime was past, his powers were failing, and he could no longer achieve those feats which to all seemed so desirable. . . . How much better, therefore, to struggle and fight, to be brave and accomplish great things, to receive the respect and applause of everyone in the camp, and finally to die gloriously at the hands of the enemy![24]

Indian children, both boys and girls, stayed close to their mothers while very young. From infancy they were taught—above all else—not to cry. A child's ill-timed squall might frighten off an unsuspecting herd of buffalo. Or worse yet, unwanted noise of any kind might endanger the whole tribe by alerting an enemy of its presence. Beyond this one restriction, Indian children were encouraged to be free spirits. Most Indians felt strongly that proper conduct was best instilled in a child through setting a good example. Marilyn Bentz, a Gros Ventre and former director of the University of Washington's American Indian Studies Program, adds:

Because parents usually did not take on disciplinary tasks, Native American societies often relied upon peer pressure to control children's behavior. In most societies, a child was a member of an extended family and was usually raised in the company of many peers. If a child did things to bring attention to himself, peers shamed him into conformity.[25]

Indian children, like children everywhere, spent most of their time at play. Their toys reflected their future roles, intended by their parents to ease their transition to adulthood—dolls and miniature tipis and travois for girls, for example, and small bows, arrows, shields, lances, and other weapons for boys. Both boys and girls also played with animal dolls, with diminutive replicas of bears, buffalo, and elks among their favorites.

Somewhere between the ages of four and seven, Indian children began learning the skills needed to take their places as productive members of the tribe. Girls were pre-

Parenting on the Plains

"Patterns of parenting in the Plains Indian community," write Mark St. Pierre and Tilda Long Soldier, *"were not so clearly defined as in Western society."* In Walking in the Sacred Manner, *the authors explain:*

"It was generally accepted that the mother's sisters would discipline and teach their sisters' children; their mother's brothers performed much the same role for boys. As [late Lakota elder] Lucy Swan once related, 'There is a lot of wisdom in this, because parents are sometimes short with their own children. The aunts and uncles could teach the children without getting upset, and that left the relationship with their mother and father a good and loving one.'

The Crow medicine woman Pretty Shield gives great insight into Indian concepts of family and parenting:
'About the time when I came to live on this world my aunt, Strikes with an Ax, lost two little girls. They had been killed by the Lakota; and so had her man. This aunt, who was my mother's sister, mourned for a long time, growing thinner and weaker, until my mother gave me to her, to heal her heart. . . .
The separation from my mother and my sisters was in fact not a very real one because the Crows come together often. . . . My aunt's lodge was large, and she lived alone until I came to stay with her. She needed me, even though I was at first too young to help her.'"

These Sioux dolls are made of leather and are accented with beads, feathers, and hair. Indian girls played with such dolls, as well as tiny tipis and travois.

pared for marriage and schooled in the work and duties of women, while boys were taught hunting skills and how to make the tools and weapons needed to meet their adult responsibilities. Instructions came not only from the children's parents but also from older youths, relatives, and tribal elders. Both girls and boys learned horsemanship and became expert riders, an essential skill in a culture so dependent upon the horse.

Horses and Buffalo

Many writers have credited the horse with having radically changed the Indians' way of life. Such an endorsement tends to overstate the horse's impact on the Indian culture. Stated more accurately, the advent of the horse *enhanced* a lifestyle that already existed by making it easier to hunt the migrating buffalo and encouraging more Indians to do so.

For example, before the horse, the Indians still hunted buffalo, but on foot with considerable risk to their personal well-being. The buffalo—or more correctly the *bison*—stood more than six feet tall and weighed up to a ton. (The term "buffalo" derives from the Spanish *bufalo*, because the early Spanish explorers mistook the bison for the wild ox of Africa and India.) David Hurst Thomas, curator of anthropology at the American Museum of Natural History, comments:

Although sometimes they hunted buffalo individually, they learned the hard way that driving a stone-tipped arrow or spear through the tough buffalo hide was no easy task. Many arrows were lost before one struck home. So the Plains Indians developed ways to take large numbers of buffalo without the dangers and uncertainties of individual stalking. . . .

Daily Life on the Plains: Families and Functions

A herd of buffalo at rest. Before the Indians acquired horses, hunting took the form of a buffalo drive: The animals were herded into chutes and then stampeded off cliffs.

The Blackfeet built what they called the *pis'kun* [pronounced PEES-kuhn](or deep blood-kettle), a huge corral of rocks, logs, or brush, constructed at the foot of a steep cliff. From the top of the bluff, directly over the *pis'kun* they laid out two lines of rock piles and brush, extending far out along the prairie, forming a huge V-shaped drive.

Led by the tribal medicine man, the Indians first herded the buffalo into the chute and then stampeded them toward the cliff.

As they reached the cliff's edge, most buffalo plunged blindly downward, into the *pis'kun*. The fall killed many outright; others were disabled with broken legs and backs. Because the barricades prevented escape, the Blackfeet could easily dispatch the living with arrows.

Archaeological evidence found throughout the Plains shows that similar buffalo drives had taken place for millenia.[26]

During the 1800s, the "dispatching" of buffalo became much easier and safer, using both bow and gun from astride a horse. The Indians could now "run the buffalo down at will, and after stripping the hides and cutting up the meat, could carry them back to the main village without difficulty."[27]

The Indian Diet

Unsurprisingly, the diet of the Plains Indians consisted mostly of buffalo meat, supplemented with small quantities of seasonal wild berries, chokecherries, turnips, and other food items obtained infrequently through intertribal or white trade. An occasional

The Bison Hunt

The bison (buffalo) were vital to the Plains Indians' survival. Hunting the huge beasts was exciting, deadly dangerous, but a source of pleasure for all, as Oglala holy man Black Elk vividly explains in Black Elk Speaks.

"We started for where the bison were. The soldier band went first, riding twenty abreast, and anybody who dared go ahead of them would get knocked off their horse. They kept order, and everybody had to obey. After them came the hunters, riding five abreast. The people came up in the rear. . . .

Then when we had come near to where the bison were, the hunters circled around them, and the cry went up, as in battle, 'Hoka hey!' which meant to charge. Then there was a great dust and everybody shouted and all the hunters went in to kill—every man for himself. They were all nearly naked, with their quivers full of arrows hanging on their left sides, and they would ride right up to a bison and shoot him behind the left shoulder. Some of the arrows would go in up to the feathers and sometimes those that struck no bones went right straight through. Everybody was very happy."

The danger of the hunt is captured in this illustration of a buffalo forcing a hunter's horse to crash to the ground.

antelope, deer, or elk from a mountain hunting excursion provided a satisfying but rare diversion from their usual fare. The nomadic tribes ate fish only when deprived of other food sources, during which times they also slaughtered their dogs and horses to sustain themselves.

Artist George Catlin, visiting an Indian tribe at the mouth of the Yellowstone River in 1832, described some of the foods he ate while spending time with the Mandan tribe:

> This is truly the land of the Epicures. We are invited by the savages to feasts of *dog's meat*, as the most honorable food that can be presented to a stranger, and glutted with the more delicious food of beavers' tails and buffaloes' tongues.[28]

Indian diets varied somewhat from tribe to tribe and place to place depending on tribal preferences and the availability of edible foodstuffs. According to the editors of Time-Life Books, the Hasinai—eight small farming tribes of the Caddoan language family in east Texas—raised bountiful crops of corn, beans, squash, sunflowers, melons, and tobacco. And they enjoyed a variety of other edibles:

> Like others at the edge of the Plains, the Hasinai were expert foragers as well as farmers. They caught fish, frogs and turtles; snared rabbits and various rodents; and took partridges, quail, wild turkeys, and waterfowl, whose calls they were adept at imitating. Among the big game in the vicinity were black bears, wild hogs, and deer, which the hunters sometimes stalked wearing the animal's hide and horns. Deer yielded venison as well as tanned skin for moccasins, leggings, shirts, skirts, and other articles of clothing; bears offered meat, fur, and fat,

which Hasinais used as ointment and sometimes quaffed as a hot drink.[29]

Typical of farming tribes, meat was secondary to the Hasinais diet. Most hunting tribes on the far reaches of the Plains, however, relied almost solely on the buffalo for food and all kinds of other necessities, including shelters, utensils, weapons, and, not least, clothing.

Indian Clothing

Indians of the plains and prairies dressed in like fashion. Men wore leggings and shirts of buckskin, often amply fringed, and robes and moccasins of buffalo hide. Also, the male was never without a breechclout, a piece of hide—usually buckskin—about twelve to eighteen inches wide by five to eight feet long. Both ends of this strip were threaded under the belt to form front and rear flaps. Plain, at first, it was later adorned with a fringe or quillwork. Women dressed in a simple strap-and-sleeve dress, usually decorated with bead- or quillwork. A cape was added for inclement weather. Knee-length leggings, gartered above or below the knee with strips of otter fur, and buckskin or buffalo hide completed their dress. Dresses and leggings were made of deer, elk, or antelope skins and were also decorated with handcrafted adornments—beads, shells, quills, fringes, the teeth and tails of animals, and suchlike.

When discussing the dress of Plains Indians, according to Josephine Paterek, an authority on the American Indian costume, several factors should be considered:

> (1) Dress had to be easily transported, readily packed, and carried with ease, particularly in the case of the nomadic tribes. (2) Vast extremes of temperatures

Plains Indians' clothing was often highly decorated, such as this Crow woman's dress studded with elk teeth.

meant that clothing must be adapted to the changes; this was usually handled by the addition or subtraction of articles of dress, but some items were of a seasonal nature. (3) Clothing was highly individualistic, reflecting not only tribal traditions but the wearer's taste and attainments. (4) Although tribal differences in dress are known, they are difficult to establish because of the continual trading, gift-giving, and intercommunication between the tribes, leading to a general similarity in Plains dress. (5) Plains costume was a costume of movement and sound—feathers and fringes streaming in the wind, tinklers and bells jangling, beads and shells rattling.[30]

Except for infrequent fur caps in winter, Indians went bareheaded on the plains throughout the year. Although hairstyles varied from shaved domes to brushlike center strips, most northern Indians opted to wear their hair long and in two braids. Unmarried women wore their braids hanging down the back and thus distinguished themselves from married women, who wore their braids in front. The majority of both men and women in the south favored a loose free-flowing hairstyle. Men particularly wore feathers in their hair. The number, size, color, and shape of the feathers varied from person to person and tribe to tribe, without adhering to any set standard or means of interpreting their symbolism.

Hairstyles, headdresses, accessories, jewelry, weapons, and face and body embellishments allowed individual expression but generally reflected distinguishing tribal characteristics. The adornment of accessories such as belts, breastplates, and utility pouches and bags for various uses, as well as weapons and shields, afforded ample opportunity for satisfying the creative urge of even the most inspired tribal artisans.

Seasonal Activities

Just as some Plains dress was seasonal, the changing seasons also strongly influenced daily life on the plains. Winter, aside from the discomforts associated with cold and inclement weather, was a time of maximum enjoyment, a respite from the pressures of war, hunting, and continual movement. The Plains Indians considered their permanent winter camp a true home. Bands, clans, and gentes reunited at a predetermined location and selected a suitable site to spend the winter, in a place appropriate to the needs of tribal members and their horses and dogs.

This 1832 painting depicts a Mandan chief wearing a decorated hide tunic and leggings as well as a long, feathered headdress.

From the first snowfall until sometime in March or April, the people settled in to savor the pleasures of home and family and the camaraderie of friends. Men hunted some and went off on occasional war and raiding parties; women, relieved temporarily from the chores of frequent moves, enjoyed spending much of their time making and repairing clothes and working at various arts and crafts. When not helping their parents, children spent their days at play. And families spent few winter nights without benefit of a tale or two spun by a tribal storyteller before a warming fire. George Bird Grinnell, who listened to many such tales, comments:

> Story telling was a favorite form of entertainment, and it was common practice for hosts at feasts to invite some story teller to be a guest, and then, after all had eaten, to relate his stories. Men known as good story tellers were in demand, and were popular.[31]

Since the Plains Indians had no written historical records, their tribal histories were passed along orally to each new generation.

Spring was a time of renewal; a time for repairing tipis and preparing to go back on the buffalo trail. Tribal hunts were held in the spring when dwindling food supplies required replenishing.

Individual family hunts were conducted throughout the summer. But much of the time was given over to festivals and ceremonial events, such as the ritualistic Sun Dance, in which "a vow is made [to the Creator] a year before the dance in return for a favor or in petition for a favor."[32]

Another tribal hunt in the autumn, followed by food and wood gathering and a flurry of preparations—drying buffalo meat, scraping hides, caching food in underground repositories, and sundry other tasks—for the approaching winter, traditionally completed the seasonal cycle.

It was a good life in the time of the buffalo. As one old warrior recalled, "Those were happy days. Our bodies were strong and our minds healthy because there was always something for both to do. When the buffalo went away we became a changed people."[33]

Character and Customs

"[My grandmother] taught me about the Four Great Virtues, which govern the conduct of the Lakota people. They are generosity, bravery, fortitude (long suffering or patience), and moral integrity."
—Madonna Swan, Lakota Holy Woman,
Walking in the Sacred Manner

The Plains Indians lived a simple life, in harmony with nature. Most of them adapted to nature's ways gracefully, surviving the difficulties and dangers of wild surroundings through their collective ingenuity, cooperation, trust in one another, and, perhaps most important, an abiding faith in a community-based religion. Osage author George E. Tinker explains:

Thus the social structures and cultural traditions of American Indian peoples are infused with a spirituality that cannot be separated from, say, picking corn or tanning hides, hunting game or making war. Nearly every human act was accompanied by attention to religious details.[34]

The Indian Way of Thinking

Perhaps no one has characterized the Native American philosophy better, and in so few words, than Jackie Yellow Tail, a young Crow woman who writes:

I think that the color of people's skin doesn't make them any better or worse than anybody else. Everybody that's here is here for a reason, whatever the Creator chose. It's what's in the person's heart and mind. There's good and bad in everybody. The positive and the negative. Mother Earth has her North Pole and the South Pole. She's got an axis [*axis mundi*, or "world axis"] that keeps her centered. The way I see it, each of us is a small replica of Mother Earth. We have our positive and our negative, and the good works with the bad. It's just that there is an imbalance in a lot of people. They go too far either one way or the other. . . .

Life is a circle, the whole world is a circle. The Christian way of seeing the world is that within this circle there's a man called Jesus; on the outside is [*sic*] the trees, the rocks, the animals; all around the world are different things that are on Mother Earth. In the center is man above all things.

The Indian way of thinking is that there is this same circle, Mother Earth, and around her are the rocks, the trees, the grass, the mountains, the birds, the four-legged, and man. Man is the same as all those other things, no greater, no less. I mean, it's all so simple; people make it so hard. That's why I say we're like Mother Earth: each one of us has that ability within us to grow spiritually, we're connected with the Creator from the top of our

Lords of the Plains

In Comanches: The Destruction of a People, *acclaimed historian T. R. Fehrenbach describes the preeminent tribes of the Great Plains, exhibiting what might be called reproachful admiration. Of thirty ethnic groups, he writes:*

"Only two peoples, the Dakotas [Sioux] and the Comanches, who were to emerge respectively as the lords of the northern and southern plains, ever numbered as many as twenty thousand. Even these great peoples, acknowledged as the most fearsome by all Amerindians around them, never mounted more than a few thousand hunter-warriors. The Shoshones who became Comanches perhaps threw five thousand warriors over the plains, but never more than a small fraction of this number at any one place or time.

Yet this handful of savages on their shaggy, many-colored ponies, in grotesque warbonnets, and with feathered lances and garish war shields, whose tents and camps were mere dots in a primordial wilderness, created the dominant image and memory of a vanished culture. The horse lifted them to riches as they understood riches and made them the most dangerous predators on the continent. . . .

The Amerindians who found the European horse and adapted it to their needs were to be those Amerindians most intransigent to further change. . . . Thus the horse did great service and great damage to the race.

The names of the horse people, however, may be those longest remembered on the continent: Dakota, Cheyenne, Kiowa, Comanche.

They stood for violence, cruelty, and blood courage—values that civilization professes to abhor. They were neither noble nor free. Yet, they will be remembered and recalled with a certain pride and nostalgia, because they also represented freedoms and values denied civilized mankind: freedom from subordination and slavery—men who took no orders except by choice, lordly creatures living as they pleased across the land. These dark-eyed hunter-killers must be remembered as long as men remain men.

For something in their lives—the hot thrill of the chase, the horses running in the wind, the lance and shield and war whoop brandished against man's fate, their defiance to the bitter end—will always pull at powerful blood memories buried in all of us."

head, our feet walk on Mother Earth. It's within us, and why should we hold that to ourselves when we know, no matter what color that person is, that he has the same spiritual yearning we have? People are a little Mother Earth, they deserve to be treated with respect. They, in turn, need to treat us with respect, that give and take, that positive and negative.[35]

Yellow Tail's musings on respecting all peoples and all things in nature, and her seeming

acceptance of the good and bad in all people, are representative of the beliefs that so greatly influenced the life paths followed by most of the Plains Indians. Empowered by such beliefs, they cultivated character traits well suited to their pathways.

Honesty and Truth

Of all the qualities desired in any culture, the Plains Indians held none more dear than honesty and truth. Marz and Nono Minor, writers and photographers of Indian lore, state:

> Honesty and truth were valued traits. There were no locks on the doors and very little theft. If one was to be gone for a length of time, a pole was put across the door to indicate the absence of the family, and no one entered the dwelling. A family, when leaving something, would put a possession marker nearby and leave it for several days, before coming back to pick it up. Truth, honesty, and the safeguarding of human life were recognized as essential to the peace and prosperity of the tribe.

> Crime was not a big problem among the Indians.[36]

Outside the tribal circle was another matter, however, as Maximilian's observation of the Mandan and Minnetaree indicates: "Some of them are addicted to thieving, especially the women and children; and it is said, that many of the Minnetarees, when they meet the Whites in the prairie, though they do not kill them, as they used to do, generally plunder them."[37]

A Loving and Caring People

Within any given Plains tribe, each individual looked after another, secure and comfortable in knowing that the entire village in turn was looking after his or her own well-being. A keen sense of mutual devotion and dependency began with the family and spread first to the village and thence to the tribe.

The Plains Indians felt a deep respect for and connection to their fellow community members and nature.

The Indian child learned early on that the good of the community always takes precedence over the good of the individual. "Children represented the continuation of society," writes Gros Ventre anthropologist Marilyn G. Bentz, "and their accomplishments signified the group's potential to endure." Bentz further notes:

In native societies, the adults primarily responsible for child care were often not the parents. In hunting and gathering societies, it was more practical for grandparents to rear children too young to participate in economic activities. For example, among such tribes as the Arapahos, Gros Ventres, Blackfeet, and Sioux of the northern plains, grandparents prepared and cooked the food, did the household chores, and took care of the children. Grandparents were also the repositories of cultural knowledge and wisdom, which they passed on to their grandchildren through instruction and stories.[38]

Children were taught from infancy to be of good nature and avoid quarrels. Such teachings, well learned, made for strong communal ties, for it is difficult not to like someone of cheerful disposition who never argues with others. Close friendships were formed in infancy and treasured from cradle to grave. And friends invariably remained steadfastly loyal to each other at the risk of life itself. This comradely attitude permeated all levels of Indian society. Their sense of communal responsibility fostered continual interplay and camaraderie. They hunted, gathered food, and ate together at a central cooking area.

"Hunger and want could not exist at one end of an Indian village or in any section of an encampment, while elsewhere there was plenty," write Marz and Nono Minor. "A successful warrior [or hunter] could not claim more than his due, but must share his hunt and gains with the less fortunate of the tribe." Moreover, as the Minors explain:

The Indians had a highly advanced concept of hospitality. It was the custom among most Indians to offer food to anyone who entered their dwelling, and to refuse was an insult. The food must be at least tasted and thanks given to the woman of the house. This was repeated at any hour of the day, and a person who visited much could be offered many meals in one day.[39]

Visitors could almost always count on preferential treatment: a favored seat by the fire, the tenderest cut of meat, the warmest place in the lodge to sleep, directly in back of the fire on a bed lined with the host's finest robes.

On the other hand, when threatened by an enemy, the Plains Indians were capable of exhibiting fierce fighting qualities, even savagery, and often did. But within their own tribal circle, they were, with few exceptions, a kind and loving people.

Social Etiquette

The Plains Indians routinely displayed their consideration for others through an elaborate system of social etiquette, seemingly odd to the uninitiated but rooted in logic. For example, a husband did not speak to his in-laws except through a third party, or by speaking his mind to an object within their earshot. This avoided direct confrontation over arguable issues and thus eliminated many arguments that might unnecessarily strain a marital relationship.

A view of camp life, as shown in an 1833 painting by Karl Bodmer. Sharing responsibility and bounty fostered a sense of community within Plains tribes.

An Indian would never disturb a conversation by walking between two people who were talking. And he never addressed people by name in their presence. To do so, he felt, weakened a relationship. Better to call a person father, brother, or friend, which served to reaffirm the person's valued relationship. Formal names were left to strangers or to those who knew the person less well. Neither would an Indian ask a stranger's name or business, feeling it more polite to wait until the natural flow of events revealed answers to such questions.

A brother and sister rarely spoke with each other and only about serious matters of immediate importance. They could never be found alone together after puberty lest they risk starting rumors of improprieties. Yet, as detached as their relationship might seem to the outsider, throughout their lives they shared an uncommon closeness. A woman's

brother exerted more influence over her future than her father; he passed judgment on her marriage suitors and assumed lifelong responsibility for her safety and protection even after she married. As a case in point, Mark St. Pierre and Tilda Long Soldier write of a Lakota courtship:

If the woman seemed interested, her suitor would approach her oldest brother and speak with him. If the oldest brother considered the young man worthy (capable of supporting a wife and family) he would give his permission. In theory a girl might end up with a man she did not care for. If, however, after a time she could not grow to care for him, she could quite easily divorce. . . .

A Lakota woman was free to act as she wished and "belonged" to no one but

An Apache bride. Some sources claim that marriages were arranged by parents and tribal officials, while others say that the suitor only needed the approval of the woman's brother.

herself. All she needed to do was place the dismissed husband's clothing outside the door, and the divorce was final.[40]

Other authorities say that Indian marriages were in fact arranged by parents, especially among leading families seeking to maintain power and prestige. "In addition to the parents, or the clan parent, of a child," writes Lenape author Jay Miller, "town [or tribal] leaders must also approve of the marriage."[41] But even when marriages were arranged, say many experts, tribal etiquette allowed the woman the right to decline a suitor's proposal.

In these ways and countless more, the Indian exhibited a deep understanding of human needs and dignity. His or her concern for others grew naturally out of a wholly interdependent society.

Respect and Responsibility

The Plains Indians respected their parents, relatives, elders, and the rights of others. They learned to live in harmony with nature and came quite naturally to think much like the wise men of the tribe, who passed along their hard-earned wisdom to their juniors. "Honor thy father and thy mother" (Exodus 20:12)—as well as all other relatives—was an obligation that most tribes observed long before white missionaries arrived on the plains. Writes historian Norman Bancroft-Hunt:

> The strongest commonly held obligation was to one's relatives, and family ties tend to emphasize the integrated nature of Plains social life. A close family, always camping together and occupying several tipis, might include grandparents, great-grandparents, unmarried brothers and sisters, parents and children; possibly totalling thirty or more individuals, each of whom had a mutually supportive role.[42]

In a few tribes, however, the aged fared less well. As Donald J. Berthrong, a professor emeritus at Purdue University and an expert on historical and legal issues related to the Cheyenne-Arapaho and other tribes, points out:

> Respect and love for elders did not deter their abandonment by some western tribes. Before acquiring horses, the Blackfeet routinely left their old, enfeebled people behind when camps moved. Elderly Kiowas were "thrown away" because those about to die were thought to be evil spirits. When non-Indians intervened to rescue such people, the "victims" were displeased because they had accepted their family's decision.[43]

Abandonment of the elderly, although it seems cruel, was a necessity considering that they lived in a harsh environment in which the lives of many perhaps depended on the deaths of a few. But after the advent of the horse travois, this practice became unneces-sary and was discontinued. Elders could then be more readily transported and were subsequently "cared for and looked after," much to the benefit of Indian youngsters. According to Bancroft-Hunt, the knowledge and experience of elders

> made them invaluable advisors to the young. A boy gained his first experience of hunting small game close to the camp under the tutelage of his grandfather, who also made him his first bow and arrows and taught him about myths and ceremonies; while grandmothers spent much of their time with the girls, beading dresses for buckskin dolls, making play tipis, and helping the mother instruct her daughter in the art of dressing and tanning animal skins. Like grandparents everywhere they spoiled the children, and there was a particularly close bond of affection between these generations.[44]

The Elderly Continue to Exert Their Influence

Most tribes, then, honored their elders, respecting both men and women for the wisdom and experience attendant to their advanced years. Many of the elderly exerted strong influence in tribal affairs and camp life, particularly old women, who were thought to hold the interests of future generations in mind. Their sometimes outspoken opinions helped to shape many tribal decisions. Writes Professor Berthrong: "Even in tribes considered male dominated, women ran camps, and political leaders were careful not to incur the displeasure of elderly women, who were capable of ridiculing a chief at public gatherings."[45]

Cleanliness

It might occur to anyone who has ever been camping that keeping clean on the plains must have been difficult. Maintaining good habits of personal hygiene was certainly not always easy for the Indians. Still, despite difficulties arising from frequent moves and inclement weather, they managed better than one might expect. Some tribes, whenever possible, bathed regularly in the morning and evening, including the Cheyenne, Crow, Sioux, and Mandan. Following his stay among the Mandan in 1833, Maximilian recorded his observations of their cleanliness:

Many of them are particularly cleanly in their persons, and bathe daily, both in winter and summer; their hands, however, are often smeared with colors and fat, nay, sometimes the whole body is bedaubed. The women are, in general, less cleanly, particularly their hands, which arises from their continual and severe labor. They generally let their nails grow long. . . . [The Mandan] bathe, in the depth of winter, in the half-frozen rivers.[46]

Of those same Mandan, George Catlin ventured that "there are few people, perhaps, who take more pains to keep their persons

An infant rests on a cradleboard in this 1896 illustration. Indian children were close to their extended families, especially grandparents, who served as affectionate mentors for the children.

Survival on the plains required Indians to stay in excellent physical health.

neat and cleanly than they do." Catlin later noted that after bathing in a nearby river the men and boys "return to their village, wipe their limbs dry, and use a profusion of bear's grease in their hair and over their bodies."[47]

Some Indians rubbed their bodies with fragrant plants and herbs. Although some tribes were less dutiful about their personal hygiene than the Mandan, Sioux, and others, most Indians kept themselves as clean as possible, if for no other reason than to stay healthy.

Health and Fitness

Since physical fitness was essential to survival on the plains, most tribes developed and implemented intensive physical training regimens. Parents and tribal elders forced Indian youths to exercise and discouraged them from adopting unhealthy or self-indulging habits. Regular fasting helped to curb obesi-

ty. Swimming and long-distance running developed strong lungs and toned the muscles. Early explorers in North America reported excellent hygiene and robust health among the native groups.

To be sure, the Indians suffered some sickness and disease. But before the Europeans arrived in the Americas—bringing smallpox, syphilis, and other Old World blights with them—good health and fitness kept the Indians virtually free from mental disorders and contagious diseases of epidemic proportions. Not so thereafter, however; according to anthropologist Henry F. Dobyns: "Thirteen known epidemics decimated native peoples in North America during the seventeenth century." And in the following century "sixteen major epidemics swept away natives in all or large portions of North America."[48] Diseases of the whites did infinitely more to decimate the Indian population than did all the guns and sabers of the U.S. cavalry.

National Characteristics

Reflecting on his travels deep into America's interior, Jonathan Carver, an early American explorer and author, later remarked on the Indians' devotion to tribe and nation. His words illuminate the collective traits of the Plains Indians as he and many of his contemporaries observed them:

> The honor of their tribe, and the welfare of their nation is the first and most predominant emotion of their hearts; and from hence proceed in a great measure all their virtues and their vices. Actuated by this, they brave every danger, endure the most exquisite torments, and expire triumphing in their fortitude, not as a personal qualification, but as a national characteristic.[49]

Certainly, the Indians' lack of a common language and failure to unite across tribal lines gravely hindered their efforts to preserve their homelands and lifestyle. Ironically, however, it was the Indians' more admirable qualities, perhaps, that hastened their own demise and the end of their way of life: Honor, truth, pride, and loyalty to family, tribe, and nation compelled them to resist the encroachment of white settlers on the plains, ushering in several decades of bloody violence.

Tribal Government

"Each band had its own chiefs, sub-chiefs, war chiefs, society leaders, clan leaders. No matter how many bands got together, they retained this parallel structure of leadership."

—James Welch, *Killing Custer*

I n general, irrespective of differences in language and geographic location, the Plains Indians shared remarkably similar ideas about leadership and government. Beyond all else, their common form of tribal government was predicated on kinship. Beginning with the band—the extended family in which everyone was related by blood, marriage, or pledge—the ties of kinship laced the entire tribe or tribal family into a unified whole.

Among the Sioux, for instance, in the words of Yankton Sioux linguist and author Ella Deloria, "The ultimate aim of Dakota life was quite simple: One must obey kinship rules; one must be a good relative."[50] Obedience to kinship rules provided a sense of individual belonging and ensured the well-being of the group.

At the same time, paradoxically, perhaps, "the American Indian was a firm *individualist*." Thus, as Thomas E. Mails observes, "it is not surprising to discover that their common form of government promoted the worth and freedom of the individual."[51]

Although some distinctions of rank were established to maintain order, there was no ruling class, as such, and virtually no class distinction. And contrary to the thinking of most whites during the nineteenth century, only rarely did a tribal chieftain hold supreme power or govern alone. As author James Welch puts it, "Chiefs were only listened to when they had a good idea."[52]

Chiefs and Lesser Chiefs

Since hunting and warring forged the tribal society and its regulating system, leadership responsibilities continually shifted and changed with the movement of game, fluctuations in population, and the acts or threatened actions of hostile tribes. Within a given tribe, depending on time and circumstance, different chiefs presided over different areas of responsibility.

Among the Crow, Assiniboin, and Cheyenne, for example, one chief would oversee the overall government of the tribe, while another chief would lead a war party, and still another, a hunting party. Some tribes would appoint a head chief and several lesser chiefs to rule individual bands and clans. And according to T. R. Fehrenbach, among the Comanches

the so-called peace chief, or band headman, was not a chief in the modern meaning of the word. . . . He was merely a recognized first among equals whose advice was often sought, and whose suggestions were usually followed. The success of such chiefs depended upon their being able to understand the tribal mood and to solve disputes in a way that impressed the collective band as being fair. The post was more an honor than true authority.[53]

When an entire Lakota tribe would assemble—usually once a year, in June—lesser chiefs would serve as the head chief's council of elders. "In the deliberations of the council," writes Robert M. Utley, a former chief historian of the National Park Service, "every decision represented consensus [general agreement], not majority vote. When consensus could not be attained, decisions were deferred or simply not made." Failure to reach agreement sometimes allowed crucial issues to go unresolved, potentially paralyzing official functions or fostering dissenting factions within the tribe. Furthermore, Utley goes on,

no family felt bound by a council's decision or a chief's instructions. Dissenters could leave at any time, to join another band or wander alone on the plains. In certain circumstances, however, everyone must obey: in wartime, during a formal camp movement, in a communal buffalo hunt involving the entire village, or in some other event affecting the com-

This 1849 painting portrays the Sioux council. Some tribal councils were made up of several lesser chiefs and led by a head chief.

mon welfare. In such undertakings, the chiefs relied heavily on men's societies. From these fraternal groups came the *akicita* [also *akecita*], or policemen, who enforced the rules and regulations laid down by the leadership.

Policies formed and actions taken at such annual gatherings helped to maintain tribal solidarity, as Utley explains:

> Likewise on the tribal level, a council of men experienced in war, the hunt, civil affairs, and spiritual matters discussed broad questions of policy, while four executive officers, "shirt wearers," carried out the policies and decisions of the council with the support of the *akicita*. For people who rarely came together as a tribe, these tribal officials, especially the shirt wearers, played an important role. They heightened awareness of tribal identity, provided a sense of tribal continuity, and dealt with increasingly difficult problems of relations of neighboring tribes.[54]

Because a chief's position was honorary and his powers advisory only, some appointees refused to accept the responsibilities of chiefdom, which entailed much work and often little appreciation.

The Making and Role of a Chief

The method of becoming a chief varied from tribe to tribe. In some tribes the title was inherited through kinship, passed along from father to son in a patrilineal society, such as that of the Omaha. When kinship descended through the mother, that is, in a matrilineal society—like the Crow society—leadership

Washakie (ca. 1804–1900) became chief of the Shoshone as a young man and kept his position for the rest of his life.

was passed through brothers and cousins. In other tribes, the Blackfeet and Cheyenne, for example, the title could be attained by brave acts; or, among the Kiowa, through wealth and influence. And in still other tribes, as with the Lakota, the choice of a chief was often based on the individual's personal attributes, such as generosity, honesty, wisdom, and the ability to lead and inspire others.

Most chiefs were veteran warriors but not necessarily old. Plenty Coups, the great Crow chieftain, for example, was twenty-three when he became chief. Washakie of the Shoshone also made chief in his early twenties. Both men retained their powers throughout their lifetimes. These men were

An 1868 treaty meeting. Treaties between Indians and whites often failed due to language barriers and the government negotiators' misconceptions of the chiefs' power.

exceptions, however, as a chief's prestige usually declined rapidly after forty, spurring wanna-be successors to clamor for his replacement at the first sign an aging chief could no longer demonstrate his ability to lead in the hunt, in war, or in making good medicine.

The duties of a camp or peace chief placed lesser physical demands on him than a chief of a hunting or war party. Hence, as in the case of the Comanche, he "was usually an older man respected for his wisdom and generosity. His role was to offer advice and to mediate disputes."[55]

Sadly, the white man's failure to understand the chief's role, his limited control, and lack of binding authority over his subjects led to the collapse of many treaties consummated between white government officials and Indian leaders. Signatory chiefs, because of language difficulties, often did not know what they were signing. Moreover, some agreed to treaty provisions without the consensus of tribal councils.

"The chiefs who signed [treaties] could not, in the loose political democracy of the Plains Indians, speak for or bind all their people to the treaty promises,"[56] writes historian Robert M. Utley. But white negotiators mistakenly believed that a chief spoke with the unanimous voice of his people.

Tribal Laws

The Plains Indians did not govern themselves by a complex system of written laws. Nor did they use judges and courts to administer justice. Adherence to tribal traditions, public opinion, and the voice of individual conscience was generally sufficient to ensure order and harmony in an Indian community. Few Indians wanted to break faith with long-standing—but unwritten—tribal conventions for regulating social conduct. But in those infrequent instances when someone broke with tradition, the offender could expect swift punishment. Indian punishment usually fit the crime.

Punishments

The following extract, compiled by George Bird Grinnell, lists a sampling of offenses deemed worthy of punishment by the Blackfeet, including their associated penalties:

Murder: A life for a life, or a heavy payment by the murderer or his relatives at the option of the murdered man's relatives. This payment was often so oppressive as to strip the murderer absolutely of his entire property.

Theft: Simply the restoration of the property taken.

Treachery (that is, when a member of the tribe went over to the enemy or gave him any aid whatever): Death on sight.

Cowardice: A man who would not fight in defense of his tribe was obliged to wear a woman's dress, and was not allowed to marry.

Rather than establishing laws, tribal councils (pictured) relied on tradition and public opinion to discourage misconduct.

Grinnell concluded: "If a man left camp to hunt buffalo by himself, thereby driving away the game, the All Comrades were sent after him, and not only brought him forcefully back, but often whipped him, tore his lodge to shreds, broke his travois, and took away his dried meat, pemmican, and other food."[57]

Capital crimes such as murder and treachery occurred only rarely among the Plains tribes and were universally dealt with harshly. The Cheyenne banished murderers from the tribe for ten years or longer before they were permitted to return. Perhaps no better example can be found than the case of Cheyenne chief Little Wolf, as told by artist/writer David Humphreys Miller, an adopted son of the Sioux. Writes Miller:

> After years of fierce struggle to win for his people the right to live in their native Montana, Little Wolf suffered deep personal tragedy. When one of his wives was seduced by a warrior named Starving Elk, Little Wolf shot him dead. Under Cheyenne law, a chief was not permitted to take offense at such an injury, and no Cheyenne could take the life of another lest the sacred arrows be blooded [defiled]. Before the council could take action, Little Wolf voluntarily accepted his punishment—permanent banishment from his people. Renouncing all rights as a chief, he was "thrown away" and never again ate or smoked with his tribesmen.[58]

Among the Crow, a killer was forced to make restitution to the victim's family. Comanche custom punished infidelity by awarding redress to the offended husband in the form of services or horses from the male offender, but only after intensive bargaining. In the main, however, the fear of strong public censure or ridicule was enough to discourage most tribal members who might be tempted to breach the laws of tradition. When milder crime deterrents failed, most Plains tribes relied on police societies to enforce tribal law.

Tribal Societies

Following family, band or clan, and tribe, Indian societies constituted the fourth vital element of the Plains Indians' life. Tribal societies took different forms: warrior, religious, healing, open and closed memberships, and so on. Some authorities on Indian culture liken these societies to such fraternal

A ceremonial skewer used in the dances of the Kaispa, or Parted-Hair Society, of the Blackfoot tribe.

Kiowan Warrior Societies

Membership in a tribal society represented the highest level of social existence among the Plains Indians. Most of these select associations were formed for religious or healing purposes but warrior societies generally became better known. In Tribes of the Southern Plains, *the editors of Time-Life Books explore some interesting particulars of several Kiowan warrior societies.*

"In Kiowa society, every little boy enrolled in a kind of school called the Rabbit Society. According to legend, the society was founded by a reclusive old man who was banished for defying his fellow tribesmen. He nearly perished in the wild, but the rabbits took pity on him, gathering food for him and teaching him their language. Once he grew wise in their ways, the rabbits suggested that he return to the Kiowa and teach the boys how to become men. He did so and was celebrated by young Kiowas thereafter as Grandfather Rabbit.

All young Rabbits in the society wore a small headdress made of elk skin and feathers and attended classes taught by their elders in horse care, hunting, and warfare; on special occasions, they feasted and danced, hopping about in imitation of their namesakes. About the age of 12, the children graduated to another society, the Herders, where their instruction continued. As they grew older, they joined war parties, at first merely to tend the horses and later to fight.

At the age of 18, a boy became a man and joined one of the warrior dancing societies, which went by such names as the Horse Headdresses and the Black Legs. Each society had its own insignia, dances, and songs and was governed by two co-leaders and two whip bearers, who supervised the activities of members. Aside from their ceremonial functions, the societies policed communal buffalo hunts and generally maintained law and order within the band."

orders as today's Elk and Moose lodges, among others, and view them as representative of the highest level of social existence among the Plains Indians. As noted by Elaine Andrews:

> Every society had its own special dances, songs, medicine bundles, and costumes. Some societies were open to all males. For example, all Blackfoot men were organized into warrior groups according to their age. Many societies, especially the military ones, were closed. A warrior was invited to join based on his courageous actions in battle. Membership in such a society was considered an honor and earned a warrior great respect.[59]

Perhaps the most famous military society among the Plains tribes was that of the so-called dog soldiers. Western writer Bruce Grant describes them as

> a member of one of the military societies of the Plains Indians, usually chosen for his bravery and fighting ability. Among the Cheyenne, the *Hotamitaneo* or Dog Society Men won such a reputation for their daring acts that the name was usually applied only to them.

> However, other tribes had Dog Soldiers, notably the Kiowa. This group was usually formed by ten picked men, who wore a black sash around their necks and swore

never to turn their faces from the enemy unless at the insistence of the entire war party. One of these men would ride ahead of the others, dismount and anchor himself to the ground by driving his lance through one end of the sash tied to his neck. He would act as a cheer leader and urge the others into battle, often dying on the spot unless his companions released him. The Kiowa called them "Chief Dogs."[60]

The Kiowa had six such warrior groups, including one with the less-than-fearsome name of Rabbits, made up of boys between ten and twelve, in training for their future role as warriors. Their unique dance resembled the hop of a rabbit. Experts believe that these societies started among the Crow, whose ranks included from four to twelve warrior groups at various times. The esteemed Crow chief Plenty Coups gave evidence of the great attraction warrior societies held for Indian youths, recalling a night when

the secret societies held meetings, the Foxes, the Warclubs, the Big-dogs, the Muddy-hands, the Fighting-bulls, and others. Bright fires blazed and crackled among the Pines, and drums were going all night long. I wished with all my heart that I might belong to one of the secret societies. I thought most of the Foxes, and I looked with longing eyes at their firelit lodge, where men spoke of things I could not know. But I was yet only a boy.[61]

Warrior societies basically served four functions: They instilled members with the satisfaction of belonging to a select group with access to special rites and privileges; they preserved order both in camp and on organized

This painting by George Catlin depicts a Sioux ritual. Societies in Plains tribes each had their own rituals, songs, and dances, and membership in such societies was a great honor.

hunts; they punished offenders of tribal law; and they fostered a martial spirit among themselves and others—particularly young males—with an end goal of ensuring tribal longevity. In exercising their limited powers, head or camp chiefs relied heavily on these groups—often referred to as police societies—as watchdogs of an orderly community.

Women's Societies

The membership of most societies comprised males only, but some all-male groups formed women's auxiliaries. Some tribes encouraged women to form their own groups, especially the village tribes of the Upper Missouri River. Writes Elaine Andrews:

> Among the Mandan and Hidatsa, for example, women were members of the Female White Buffalo Society. The dances the women performed were meant to attract the buffalo to the hunters. Since the well-being of the entire tribe depended on successful buffalo hunts, the Female White Buffalo Society was very important. Only the most respected women were allowed to join.[62]

The purposes of most societies were generally rooted in religious belief and practice or in healing the sick and treating the injured. Members of these various orders often served as advisers to tribal chiefs and councils and exerted strong influence over tribal affairs.

In sum, then, the tribal government of the typical Plains tribe embodied a chief or chiefs, a council of elders or shirt wearers, various societies, and lastly—since it was a democratic form of government—all the remaining people of the tribe.

Religion and Medicine

"The word Wakan-Tanka . . . means literally 'the great mystery' and is a metaphor for the very mysterious forces that caused the universe to come into creation. It has aspects that reflect both male and female traits. All of creation, the Rock, Four Winds, the Sky, Mother Earth, the Sun, Moon, Lightning, the Human, Buffalo, Bear, and Plant and Animal Nations are aspects of Wakon-Tonka [*sic*]."

—Mark St. Pierre and Tilda Long Soldier, *Walking in the Sacred Manner*

The Lakota called the creative power in whom they trusted Wakan-Tanka, the Great Spirit or Great Mystery. Sometimes mistakenly translated as God, Wakan-Tanka does not refer to a god character to whom male characteristics are often assigned, such as Yahweh of the Old Testament, but rather to an unknown supreme power or force responsible for creating the universe and everything in it.

The Crow personified the force as the First Maker, whereas the Pawnee referred to it as Ti-rá-wa. The Arapaho also personified the power as the Man-Above. Each tribe knew their creator by a different name. Some thought that He resided in the sun and radiated His warmth and power in its rays. But whatever they believed or chose to call either their god or creative force, religion permeated every aspect of the Plains Indians' being and influenced everything they did.

A mother in Montana holds her baby up to be blessed by the rising sun, regarded as a symbol of the Supreme Being.

Success in a venture or victory in war could not be achieved without divine assistance. Thus the Indians actively sought the favor of the force that ruled nature by working *through* nature. They believed, for instance, that by wearing clothes made from the skins of animals, they were transmitting life from the animal to themselves so that they might live. Not only were they exhibiting a closeness to another of nature's creations, they were also preserving a semblance of the animal. They often rode into battle wearing the skin of a fierce animal or some bird of prey, as an appeal to their Creator for help, hoping to acquire the traits of the animals whose skin they wore.

The Indians' reverence toward a Supreme Being or Power could be seen in the circular arrangement of their tipis in an encampment, in which they left an opening facing east for the morning sun to greet them. The sun's rays reminded them to start each day with a prayer. Their god was all-powerful and present everywhere. They worshiped Him both individually and communally. They built no churches, however, for their god was within every individual and among every group. Although authorities today generally categorize Native American religions as monotheistic—that is, based on the worship of a single god—the Plains Indians honored a variety of lesser gods or powers.

Oneness

Lesser gods or powers might be defined as those entities to whom the Supreme Being entrusted much of the secondary labor of creation. These subordinate deities included Sky Father and Earth Mother, revered by the Sioux, Cheyenne, Arapaho, and others; the sun, moon, and stars, which figured in virtually all Plains religions; the Four Sacred Powers of the Cheyenne—symbolized by the Four Directions—who directed the winds, rains, and seasons and infused all people with the breath of life, and many other elements of nature essential to their existence.

Four Directions or Four Winds symbolism was Plains-wide. Among the Sioux, for instance, according to Mark St. Pierre and Tilda Long Soldier, "in the sweat lodge, as in all Lakota ceremonies, the wisdom and help of the four directions—winds—are called upon by name for help and wisdom."[63] While the Four Directions or Winds were conceived as separate entities, they were addressed as one Power.

Although the Indians paid tribute to these lesser gods, they held firmly to their belief in a single Creator of all things. When tornadoes, flash floods, blizzards, and the like occurred, they could direct their few fault-findings toward the lesser gods. This enabled them to preserve an untarnished relationship with the one Ultimate Being—an eternal god without beginning or end—who promised them life ever after in the next world.

The Indians' belief in an overriding Great Spirit and an afterlife is not unlike the convictions of Christians and members of various other world religions. Perhaps the major difference between Native American religions and Christianity or other monotheistic theologies lies in the Indians' seemingly heightened sensitivity to the natural forces surrounding all of humankind. Witness, in part, how Cheyenne-Arapaho John Redtail Freesoul perceives the religion of his Native American people:

> There is no philosophy or dogma or doctrine with us. We don't separate religion and culture. Our way of life is life itself, a living relationship and a living realization. . . . The Great Spirit is male and female. The male aspect of the Great Spirit is Sky Father, the female aspect is Earth Mother. All life is the child of Earth Mother and Sky Father. As sons and daughters of the earth and sky, we are all related, not

This 1939 photo shows a man emerging from a sweat lodge. The Sioux used steam baths to summon wisdom and assistance from the Four Directions.

only to all races but also to plants, animals, and rocks. They are our relatives.

All life is subject to the "natural law" of the Great Spirit, which is order, balance, and harmony. Regardless of race or ideology, the sun sets in the west and rises in the east, on the Communist, the Catholic, the Anglo, and the Indian. The effects of the four seasons are experienced by the aspen, the eagle, the four-legged and the two-legged. All life is one with the same Source, even though there are differences and each is unique. This is one reason why we call the Great Spirit "the Great Mystery.". . . We are stewards, temporarily here to caretake the body we live in and the earth we live on, to fulfill our vision and individual destiny in harmony with one another and in balance with nature.[64]

Many Indian writings express views similar to those of Freesoul that plainly speak to the holistic quality underlying many, if not all, Native American religions; that is, belief in the total interaction of humankind and environment yields a religion greater than the sum of its parts. And a people at one with their Creator and the universe.

The Vision Quest

John Redtail Freesoul wrote of fulfilling a vision. Dreams and visions played a key role in the lives and religious beliefs of the Plains Indians, providing the dreamer or vision seeker with a line of communication to the spirit world. Whereas a dream may occur without conscious effort on the part of a dreamer, a vision is usually actively induced by questing. Arlene Hirschfelder and Paulette Molin, widely recognized authorities on Native American religions, define a vision quest as

the ritual seeking of communication with the spirit world by a solitary individual. It

The Sacred Pipe

Among the Sioux, Cheyenne, and other Plains tribes, the sacred pipe represents a symbolic channel to the spirit world. "With the smoking of the first sacred pipe," writes John Redtail Freesoul, "the ancient Native American elders of this continent discovered in spiritual communion that to share breath is to share life." In Breath of the Invisible: The Way of the Pipe, *Freesoul shares some of his knowledge of the pipe and what it means to the Indian.*

"The sacred pipe is many things. . . . There are specific clan, society, personal, social, and council pipes. There are sun dance pipes, marriage pipes, and war pipes. There are pipe dances.

The prayer pipe is a ceremonial tool and a traveling altar. While leaning against a forked peg pressed and anchored in the earth, the pipe becomes a center of focus and concentration—an altar, similar to a

A Sioux pipe in the form of a seated woman. The Plains Indians considered the pipe a link to the spiritual world.

mandala [a Hindu or Buddhist graphic symbol of the universe]. . . .

The pipe is used in all Plains Native American ceremonies. It is the center of all we do; it is the 'axis mundi' [world axis] which forms a bridge between earth and sky, the visible and the invisible, the physical and the spiritual. The sacred pipe was brought to different tribes through different messengers, for the invisible spirit world is widely populated, as is the visible world. To the Blackfoot it was Thunder who brought the pipe, to the Arapahoe it was Duck. To many tribes it was White Buffalo Calf Maiden. It was the prophet Sweet Medicine who brought the arrow pipe bundle to the Cheyennes. . . .

The owner of a pipe bundle is sometimes known as a pipe holder or carrier. . . . A pipe holder is respected as one whose priority in life is purity, and is thus requested by people to conduct ceremonies with the pipe. This is a sacred responsibility. A pipe holder is expected to observe a code of purity in feelings, words, and deeds.

The pipe and all that it symbolizes is part of the Native American view of life. The Source and center of all existence is pure spirit existing in all created things simultaneously as Great Spirit. . . .

All that exists is alive. All that exists is related, sharing a common Source, a common breath. Plants, animals, rocks, and people breathe. The earth breathes. Earth Mother or Nature is the Creator's breath made visible. When there is concentration on, attention to, and recognition of this reality while one is smoking a prayer pipe, then a powerful transformation occurs. The smoke becomes sacred. The spirit of God in us all becomes visible as sacred smoke."

is conducted in an undisturbed natural setting, often at a site sacred to the tribal group. Generally, the individual ritually prepares under the guidance of one or more medicine people. Vision quest rites vary from one tribal culture to another with differences including age, gender, and other elements. It may take place once at adolescence, repeatedly as part of a long-term training in puberty, at adolescence and in adulthood or in maturity only. In many cultures the vision quest is associated only with males, but in others females may also undergo the rite. The length of time an individual undertakes a vision quest also varies[;] many last from one to four days. Ritual elements identified in many cultures include praying with the sacred pipe, fasting from food or water and taking offerings of tobacco, pieces of flesh or other sacred gifts to the spirits. A vision quest may be undertaken for a number of reasons: to complete a puberty ceremony, to prepare for becoming a healer or shaman, to fulfill a vow, to participate in other ceremonies and/or to seek spiritual guidance in his or her life.[65]

The vision seeker often underwent a preliminary purification rite in preparation for a vision quest. Rites varied from tribe to tribe but involved emptying the body of all poisons and excesses by bathing, sweat baths, herbal drinks that induced vomiting, and numerous other methods. Spiritual cleansing usually required adhering to a special diet and abstaining from sexual relations.

After preparing themselves, vision seekers usually retired to a remote place, often in high, rugged country, the closer to the Supreme Power the better. "At the spot of seeking, they built beds of flat rocks, sometimes covering them with pine branches or with sweet sage and ground cedar—all materials which had sacred qualities," writes Thomas E. Mails. "They also made physical sacrifices of the flesh, which they believed represented ignorance, and began praying."[66] A quest usually lasted about four days, during which time the vision seeker neither ate nor drank but prayed—or as the Sioux say, "lamented"—continuously.

When a quester's "laments" were answered, seekers were rewarded with a vision or voice message from supernatural powers that sometimes guided them thereafter for a lifetime. Those whose quests went unanswered by the spirits occasionally borrowed or bought the use of someone else's vision. Sometimes many years elapsed before the meaning of a spiritual message became clear, generally with the help of a medicine man. The vision's recipient then put together a medicine bag or pouch.

The medicine bag contained one or more objects considered sacred by the individual—animal bones, tobacco, spices, and the like—and thought to possess spiritual power. For the rest of his or her life, the bag's owner would call on that personal power to bring success in hunting and war, long life, spiritual guidance, and countless other life-enhancing aids.

Some vision questers experienced more than one vision—a sign of special gifts—and went on to become medicine men or healers. Medicine men, or shamans, as they were called, acted as intermediaries to the spirit world, guided religious ceremonies, and practiced spiritual healing.

Medicine Men and Healers

"Some men among the Arapaho, and among other Indians, had special gifts," recalls

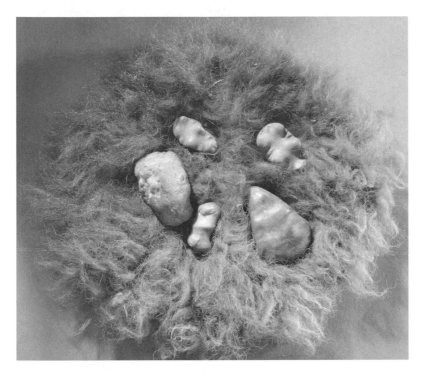

These buffalo stones were kept in a medicine bundle and used in Blackfoot rituals to call buffalo. The objects in medicine bags were also thought to bring success in war and spirituality.

Althea Bass in *The Arapaho Way: A Memoir of an Indian Boyhood*, as quoted by Thomas E. Mails.

> They knew, each one of them, everything connected with some of our ceremonies; they knew songs and rituals for healing the sick and for bringing success in war and hunting, for bringing rain, and for warding off storms. They performed these services for anyone in need of them, or for a whole village, and sometimes for the whole tribe.[67]

Non-Indians call these practitioners of spirituality and healing by any number of different names—medicine men or women, shamans, priests, caciques, singers, herbalists, healers, and others—but these terms are foreign to Indian tongues. Each Indian language had its own term for the practitioners of medicine and the healing arts, which translates into such titles as priest and doctor. Whites generally believed the practices of medicine and healing to be the same, but many tribes distinguished one from the other.

According to Carl Waldman, author of several acclaimed books on Native Americans, the term *medicine* itself means "in general, the mysterious power inherent in the universe; more specifically, power that cures the sick, or the object or substance itself that effects change or healing."[68]

Among the Pawnee and other tribes, the *priest* acted as an intermediary through whom the Creator channeled His power and wisdom—that is, His *medicine*—to minister to individuals or to influence events, much like a present-day pastor or priest. He conducted religious rites and dances and used his powers to control supernatural forces for the benefit of his people. The Pawnee priesthood, but not all others, was hereditary and descended to the next male kin in the maternal line.

The duties of the *doctor* or herbalist compared to those of today's doctor or physician, except that the Indian doctor healed with herbs and potions and by banishing evil spirits. Blackfoot doctors held their remedies in strict secrecy, ostensibly out of superstition but possibly to ensure job security. Cheyenne and Kiowa doctors practiced internal medicine and even minor surgery with great success, but most doctors rarely attempted surgery.

When Indians fell ill they usually sought a cure first from the healing powers of a personal medicine bundle—a hide- or cloth-wrapped package or box containing one or more objects or materials considered to be sacred and to possess spiritual power. If this failed, a doctor was summoned. Failing all else, a priest was called to invoke his power and knowledge of the supernatural.

Doctors dressed fairly conservatively when attending the ill—usually wearing a breechclout or everyday garb, sometimes augmented by special headgear and assorted rattles, charms, and gadgets. In contrast, the priest usually dressed differently from others, in a highly individualistic manner. George Catlin described a Blackfoot priest as wearing a buffalo horn headdress, as well as

the strangest medley and mixture, perhaps[,] of the mysteries of the animal and vegetable kingdoms that ever was seen. Besides the skin of the yellow bear . . . there were also the skins of snakes, and frogs, and bats,—beaks and toes and tails of birds,—hoofs of deer, goats, and antelopes; and, in fact, the "odds and ends," and fag ends, and tails, and tips of almost anything that swims, flies, or runs, in this part of the wide world.[69]

Or a priest might typically wear, as writers and photographers Marz and Nono Minor describe, "a bearskin reaching from heels to head, covering the head" and at another time he "might wear a costume of finest beadwork or quill work, decorated with much fringe, and a horned bonnet or turban headdress of wolfskin."[70]

The nature of an illness often determined whether a doctor or a priest was called to attend a sick person. As Navajo anthropologist Jennie R. Joe points out, most Native American healers

utilize a variety of treatment modalities [forms], depending on whether the source of the illness is natural or supernatural. In addition, there are other important specialists or subspecialists in most tribes— herbalists, midwives, and diagnosticians. Some aid the healers, and others practice independently and may be called upon because of their expertise in such procedures as setting bones, treating wounds, making diagnoses, assisting with births, and making herbal medicines.

"Comparable to priests or ministers, indigenous healers not only are sought in time of illness," adds Joe, "but also are utilized to ensure protection or to bless a happy occasion."[71] Depending on the tribe, the type of illness, and the kind of treatment, a healing ceremony usually lasted for only a few minutes in simple cases but extended for as long as a year or two in complex cases that required multiple ceremonies.

Theories of Disease and Treatment Techniques

The Plains Indians understood disease in spiritual terms. They believed in the unity and interaction of body, mind, and spirit.

"Not only must humans, viewed as only one part of creation, and all the elements of the natural world be in balance, but people and the spirit world must also be in harmony," write authors Hirschfelder and Molin. "Disease and illness result from a lack of harmony, balance, or equilibrium between the sick person and his or her surroundings."[72]

Most tribes traditionally attributed disease to spiritual causes. While the treatment of injuries, wounds, broken bones, and the like might receive obvious practical treatments, without ritual, tribal healers relied on herbs and other natural elements and ceremony to treat spiritually induced illnesses.

Blackfoot herbalists are known to have used thirty-four different herbs in treating common ailments such as colds, stomach problems, eye diseases, snow blindness, and snake and rabid animal bites. "There are hundreds of cures set forth in literature by and about Indians," notes Thomas E. Mails,

Doctors of the Plains Indians used rattles and other objects and administered herbal remedies to heal patients and rid them of evil spirits.

The Sun Dance

The Plains Indians often subjected themselves to rituals of self-induced pain and suffering as a way of demonstrating the sincerity of their belief in the spirits. One such ritual was the Sun Dance ceremony, a colorful and dramatic spectacle in which the entire tribe participated. In Killing Custer, Blackfoot–Gros Ventre author James Welch describes the tribal spectacle:

"A holy man, experienced and honored by the people, selected the right rustling-leaf tree for the lodgepole, the centerpiece of the ceremony. . . .

At the Sun Dance site . . . warriors stripped the holy tree of its lower limbs and painted it blue, green, yellow, and red, each

During the Sun Dance, a Blackfoot brave leans back, pulling on the sticks that pierce his chest.

color symbolizing one of the four horizontal directions. They built an arbor of willows and cottonwoods to provide shade against the burning sun [for the dance usually took place in June or July]."

After participating warriors had purified themselves and offered prayers to the Great Mystery, and the holy man had filled the sacred pipe and invoked the help of a host of spirits, the people raised the rustling-leaf tree, then, continues Welch:

"They built a circle around it of twenty-eight forked posts, and from each post they placed a long pole which was bound high up in the medicine tree. . . . At last the structure was a lodge and the lodge was built to honor the sun. . . .

Some of the men vowed to undergo the piercing ceremony, to dance before the pole, to endure terrible pain to expiate sins, to control passions, to enter the spiritual realm of Wakan Tanka.

The most common form of piercing was through the breast. Two sticks pierced the breast, one on each side, then were fastened to rawhide strings that hung from the medicine tree. The warrior danced, sage tied around his wrists and ankles, sage wreath around his head, blowing an eagle-bone whistle, leaning back away from the tree until the strings were taut. Then he danced some more to the fast drumming, and more still, until at last, mercifully, the skin ripped and the sticks broke free and he fell to the ground, released from his past transgressions or in fulfillment of his vow to the Grandfather, Wakan Tanka. . . . After a succession of complex rituals, a medicine woman, who had handled the sacred pipe during the proceedings, gave it to the pipe keeper, who offered up more prayers and gave thanks to Wakan Tanka, thus ending the four-day ceremony."

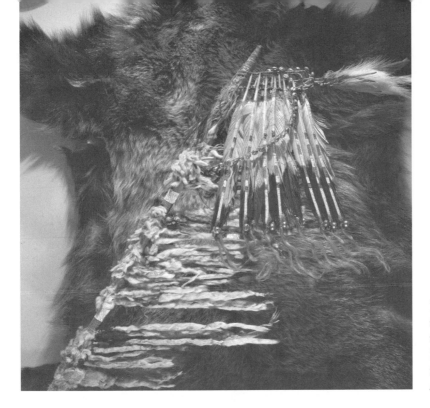

This Blackfoot pipe was kept in a medicine bag. It was thought to be a gift from Thunder and to protect the tribe from enemies and sickness.

"and more than enough to substantiate their superb healing abilities."[73]

The Indian spiritual healer thought of himself as a "tube" between the Great Spirit and his patient, often spending several days preparing himself before offering treatment to the sick person. Mails likens the preparations of the Plains healers to those of the present-day Hopi of Arizona. During the preparatory period "they work feverishly through prayer and meditation to cleanse themselves; to get the 'me' or self which impedes God out of the way so that they can be clear, clean, fit channels through which the Great Spirit can and will work."[74]

The most common primitive theory of disease held that most illnesses were caused by a foreign object or entity in the body. The Shoshone, for example, thought disease was caused by a ghost entering a person's body. In some tribes a shaman called a sucking doctor would attempt to heal the patient by sucking out the evil or foreign entity with his mouth or with a sucking tube. A shaman would sometimes hide a stone or other object in his mouth and later spit it out and claim it as the cause of the malady.

Cheyenne doctors often spat chewed herbs on the patient's body. Another technique called for breathing or blowing on some part of the body corresponding with the internal affliction. One Kiowa doctor closed wounds using a wooden suction cup and melted buffalo tallow. A Crow doctor once used a pipe stem to suck a bone, a black beetle, and a chunk of meat from a patient.

The Indians used everything possible to harness supernatural powers and combat illness and disease, including visions, songs, dances, chants, medicine bags and bundles, sacred pipe rituals and Sun Dance ceremonies, and all sorts of accoutrements: sacred flutes, rattles, bows, arrows, shields, bear claws, eagle talons, and many more. Although

A depiction of a Mandan cemetery, painted by George Catlin, reveals a circle of skulls in front of corpses on scaffolds.

they handled minor ailments remarkably well within the limits of their native medical techniques, in most cases of serious injury or illness, the patient usually died.

Death and Afterlife

The Plains Indians shared a near-universal belief in some form of afterlife, but their conception of what happened to a human at death and beyond varied from one tribe to another. Many tribes, for example, thought that an individual possessed at least two souls; one gave life to the body, the other traveled in dreams and visions. Some tribes such as the Mandan and Sioux believed that humans have four souls. Howard L. Harrod, who has lectured and written extensively in the fields of sociology of religion and Native American religions, writes of the Mandan:

Mandans thought that humans possessed four spirits. A white spirit was associated with the white sage plant. The second spirit was light brown and was associated with the meadowlark. The third spirit was identified more closely with the particular dwelling place of the dead person. The fourth spirit was black and was associated with a ghost that might frighten the people. The white and brown spirits united after death, traveling to the village of the dead, while the third spirit remained near the lodge where the person had died. [75]

Most Plains Indians—the Sioux, Blackfeet, Mandan, Gros Ventre, and Arapaho, to name a few—placed their dead on a scaffold or in a tree. The Kiowa interred their dead in caves and under rock piles, however, as did other southern tribes. After the deceased were properly attended to, all tribes observed a mourning period. But mourning customs

"Other-Side Camps"

The Plains Indians envisioned the afterlife in different ways. As quoted by Mark St. Pierre and Tilda Long Soldier in Walking in the Sacred Manner, *Jackie Yellow Tail describes the Crow perception of the place where people go at death.*

"We call the place you go at death the 'Other-side Camps.' That's the closest translation I could come to. I don't think there is a word for 'hell' in our native language. There is no word for 'devil.' Some people call it the 'Happy Hunting Grounds,' but we Crow call it the 'Other-side Camps.' It is the next spiritual plane.

When our people are dying, the people from the Other-side come to get them. They take them to be with the loved ones who have gone on before. It is a loved one, a favorite grandma or perhaps grandpa, who comes to speak with them and tell them their time is near. We consider this to be a blessing."

The Crow interred their dead in trees (pictured). When people died, according to Crow belief, they were visited by the spirits of deceased relatives.

otherwise varied on the plains, as author Bruce Grant indicates:

> Mourning the dead was customary. Among a few tribes the name of the dead person was never mentioned. Others observed the mourning period by cutting off their hair, wailing loudly, throwing away all ornaments and neglecting their persons, or carrying around a bundle representing the deceased. Cheyenne widows slashed their arms and legs.[76]

The deceased's soul was thought by all Plains people to travel to the land of the dead, but the Indians' concept of the afterworld also varied from tribe to tribe. For example, explains Howard L. Harrod,

> the land of the dead was imagined in very different ways, but in many instances spirits lived there in much the same way as they had in the land of the living. For the Blackfeet, this land was in the Sand Hills, a place somewhere out on the plains away from the camps of the living.

Some Hidatsas thought it was under Devil Lake in North Dakota, while others thought there was a sky country where the dead lived again.

"Indigenous traditions about death still persist among the Northern Cheyenne," who believe, asserts Harrod, that "the spirits of most people who die travel to a land of the dead located at the end of the Milky Way."[77]

Not all tribes believed the afterworld to be a happy place where the spirit lived in much the same way as the person had lived in the world. A few tribes, such as the Blackfeet and Gros Ventre, envisioned only a bleak afterlife where ghostly figures endured a timeless state of melancholy.

No matter how the Indians perceived eternity, their belief in an afterlife was unshakable. Author Frank B. Linderman, who has closely observed and written about many Indians, concurs: "There is never any shadow of doubt in . . . expressions by old Indians concerning death and a future life. They do not merely imply belief, but carry the positive declaration, 'I know!' "[78]

6 Arts, Crafts, Games, and Storytelling

"A people without history is like wind on the buffalo grass."
>—Old Lakota saying (quoted in Russell Freedman, *The Life and Death of Crazy Horse*)

Much of what we know today about the history of the Plains Indians can be traced back in time through the wonder of their art and legends. All forms of their arts and crafts imitated life and utilized the animal, vegetable, and mineral components of nature. "Native Americans regard art as an element of life, not as a separate aesthetic expression," writes Phoebe Farris-Dufrene, a Powhatan and associate professor of art and design at Purdue University. "Art, beauty, and spirituality are intertwined in the Native American routine of living,"[79] she adds.

Thomas E. Mails, who has spent years chronicling Indian cultures in words and pictures, shares Farris-Dufrene's views. Comments Mails:

The Plains Indians' craftworks, including their weapons, were a result of what they had been shown in dreams and visions, and as such were in themselves a link with the Supreme Being. Something about the form and decoration of each piece always moved its owner beyond its earthly purpose. In a sense, considering the attitude and care employed in making any object, it may be said that he prayed his creations into their finished form. Thus it was inevitable that the piece he produced always enshrined each man in his heaven-earth relationship.

"And by the time he died," declares Mails, "much of the story of his life could be read in the sum of the pieces he left behind."[80]

Painting and Pictographs

The Plains Indians obtained paint from the natural elements of their surroundings. "They used fine clays containing different oxides of iron," notes author Bruce Grant. "These they mixed with bear grease or buffalo tallow." They used blood and they prized the hard, yellow substance found in the buffalo's gallbladder. "The Sioux used bulberries, a plant like sumac," adds Grant. "Flowers, barks, and other vegetable matter also provided paints and coloring."[81] The Indians also called on nature to supply the tools essential to their art.

According to Carl Waldman, lexicographer of Indian lore and culture, Native American painting techniques included

applying paint with fingers; with pieces of chalk, charcoal, or clay; with wood, bark, or reeds softened at the ends; or with bones, especially the spongy knee joint of the buffalo; and sometimes spraying it on with their mouths. Shells and pottery were used as paint cups. Horses, dwellings, totem poles, masks, pottery, bags, and other objects were painted ceremonially.[82]

Painting, next to preparing and sewing skins, represents the oldest of all Indian arts and crafts, dating back to at least prehistoric times. For some four thousand years before Europeans landed in North America, Indians were painting the walls of caves, cliffs, and river canyons. Their rock paintings took the form of giant pictographs—a pictograph is a picture or sign representing a word or idea as opposed to a sound—and are called petroglyphs.

Most Indian art, of course, was accomplished on a much smaller scale. Tipi coverings provided the most popular outlet for male creativity, while females favored painting rawhide parfleche storage and carrying cases and similar items. The buffalo robe was the next most popular item for painting with both men and women. The art on women's

robes often "featured geometric designs such as the box and border" or "the hourglass and border," whereas men's robes typically depicted a motif known as the "feathered circle" or the "black bonnet," depicted by concentric circles with emanating radials. Men also wore an "exploit robe" showing a record of the wearer's war deeds in pictographs consisting "of stylized figures in battle scenes with many warriors, horses, and other animals."[83]

Indian art evolved over the years, of course, especially following the arrival of Europeans in North America. As Phoebe Farris-Dufrene points out: "Greater naturalism in the depiction of people occurred in the mid-1890s as a result of interaction with European and American artists such as Karl Bodmer and George Catlin." Yet Native American artists have retained a simplicity and grace in their work that uniquely reflects their culture and heritage. Writes Farris-Dufrene, in summation: "Native American

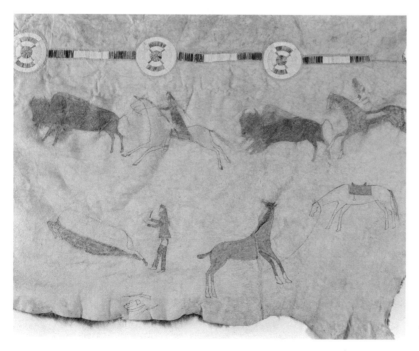

A Shoshone hunter recorded his success in this buffalo robe painting from about 1875. The quillwork strip features the "feathered circle" motif.

thinking has not ever separated art from life, what is beautiful from what is functional. . . . The Native American aesthetic has survived colonialism, servitude, racial discrimination, and rapid technological change."[84]

Face and Body Painting

The Indian painted his face and body for ceremonial purposes, for protection against the elements, insects, and enemies, and to strike fear in his foes. Indians favored red in decorating their faces and bodies for battle. "It is possible Indians were first called 'red men' or 'Redskins' by whites because they often used red paint, a symbol of strength and success for many tribes,"[85] theorizes Carl Waldman. A more popular view, however, attributes the derivation of such names to the Indians' skin color.

In their face and body art, as in all their artwork, the Indians commonly followed a definite theme, with specific meanings implicit in each color and design. Such meanings varied, however, from tribe to tribe. As Bruce Grant briefly explains:

> War paint among the Plains Indians, for instance, might be an excessive use of any color. White stood for mourning, black for joy, and red for happiness and beauty. The Cheyenne used rings and stripes of different colors when going to war, and on returning they used only black to indicate their joy at arriving back safely. The Cherokee, on the other hand, used red for success, blue for defeat or trouble, black meant death, and white, peace and happiness.[86]

By and large, red dominated Indian color schemes for body art and was also widely

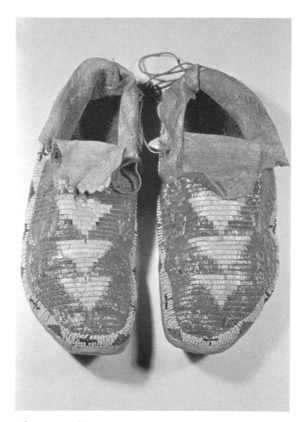

This pair of Sioux mocassins is decorated with intricate quillwork in a geometric pattern.

used for decorating war ponies, lances, shields, and ceremonial articles. Women occasionally painted themselves to enhance their beauty, but more sparingly so than men.

Quillwork and Beadwork

Quillwork—that is, the act, method, or end product of work using bird or porcupine quills, such as embroidery or weaving—preceded beadwork and represented what was probably the highest achievement of the female arts. Indian lore lexicographer John Stoutenburgh Jr. includes this concise description of the quillworking process in his informative dictionary:

A Fox beadworker. Europeans brought beads to the plains in the late 1700s, and beadworking gradually replaced quillworking as the predominant female art.

Quills were died with the juice from berries, etc. They were flattened between the teeth when they were needed for use. They were also softened with hot water and then flattened with rocks. They were laced into moccasins, shirts, pipe covers and any number of articles.[87]

The chief quillworking tribes among the Plains Indians were the Cree, Sioux, Cheyenne, and Arapaho. In early times porcupine quillwork formed an important part of garment decoration, but as Indian costume authority Josephine Paterek points out:

Much work was done with bird quills, especially when green was desired, for they took dyes better. Red and yellow colors were fairly easily obtained. Black was often introduced by the use of maidenhair ferns. Designs were simple and geometric, typically done in a two-thread sewing technique.

When European traders arrived on the plains bringing beads in the late 1700s, the Indians began developing beadworking skills. For a time the Indians practiced both quillworking and beadworking, but beadworking gained dominance by the 1830s. Continues Paterek:

The late 1800s produced such a proliferation of beadwork that often entire garments were covered with beads, especially vests, moccasins, and leggings. In the early stages beadwork continued with the geometric designs of quillwork; later, the floral designs of the Northeastern Indians were adopted. The first major type of bead was the "pony bead," brought in by traders on their ponies. The smaller seed beads in a great variety of colors appeared around 1840, followed by the medium-sized, often faceted, beads of the 1870s.[88]

As in Native American artwork, Indian beadworkers—most of whom were and continue to be women—incorporated individualism and readily identifiable tribal or mystical themes into their designs. Experts generally characterize the years from 1860 to 1900 as the period of greatest Indian achievement in beadworking artistry. After the turn of the century, the beadworkers' highly developed skills, previously passed down from one generation to the next, declined and all but disappeared for a time. Recently, however, a rekindled interest in beadwork among some tribes suggests that a new generation of artisans might emerge to recapture old skills and breathe new life into a dying art.

Utensils and Tools

The Plains Indians handcrafted nearly every utensil, tool, or miscellaneous article essential to their lifestyle and longevity. Everything they fashioned by hand with painstaking care served a useful purpose. No item or accessory was irrelevant. In their perpetual wanderings, they could own only what they could carry. "Every object served a three-fold function," writes Thomas E. Mails. "The first was to intensify the artist's spiritual feelings, the second was to play a utilitarian role in personal and community life, and the third was to be both mobile and durable."[89] Clearly, in meeting these criteria, the Plains people demonstrated rare ingenuity, versatility, and craftsmanship.

According to Marz and Nono Minor, writers specializing in Indian crafts, household items varied with tribal locations:

Baby beds were sometimes constructed on the plan of a portable box and adapted to the age of the child. . . .

Wood, pottery, baskets, and bone were all used for spoons and bowls [although pottery was used only rarely on the plains]. . . . If a spoon or other dish was highly decorated, it was usually used for ceremonial purposes and was a treasured heirloom, passed on through the family and tribe.

Most Indian tribes had central cooking and a large dish for the main meal, with smaller dishes to hold salt and condiments. All could come and eat from the tribal cooking pot. The meal was usually served on a tray large enough for the entire tribe and piled with corn, other vegetables, and fish or game. . . .

Brooms made of coarse grass or twigs were used to sweep the home, and a brush from a bird wing was used to keep the central firepit clean. Many Plains tribes and those of the Rocky Mountains used a wooden spade-like implement to remove snow from the ground near the entrance of the lodge.[90]

Before traders introduced metal tools to the plains, the Indians fashioned virtually all of their work implements from bone, wood, and stone. For pounding berries or grain against a flat stone slab, or for breaking up bones to extract the marrow, Indian women used a hammer called a berrymasher, made by lashing a stone head to a wooden handle with rawhide. Small shale slabs or water-tumbled pebbles served as scrapers, and efficient knives were honed from stone and bone. Awls, used for punching holes in the process of sewing skins together with rawhide sinew, were also made of bone.

Picks crafted from deer and buffalo bones made excellent digging implements, as did hoes made from the shoulder blades of buffalo. The list goes on. Suffice to say again, however, that by the judicious and inventive use of their natural resources the Plains Indians were able to make, shape, or fashion every utensil and tool necessary to sustain their life on the plains.

Games and Sports

Beyond devoting most of their energies to simply staying alive in the wilderness, the Plains Indians still found sufficient time and leftover vitality for play. Indians loved playing games and enjoyed sporting competition. According to Marz and Nono Minor, "most [Indian] games fell into two categories, those of chance, and those of dexterity." The Minors explain:

Games of chance were of two types: those games in which implements, such as dice, were thrown at random to determine a number or numbers, the sum of the count being kept by means of sticks, pebbles, or bits of bone; and those in which one or more players guessed in which of two or more places something was concealed, with success or failure resulting in the gain or loss of counters.

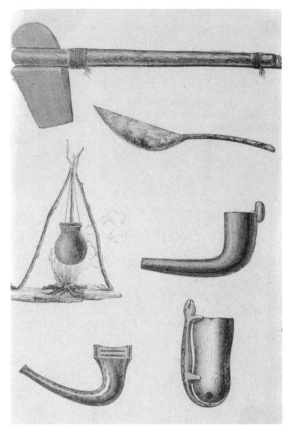

An array of Indian tools (from top to bottom): an ax, a spoon, a kettle, and three pipes. Before metal was introduced to the plains, utensils were made of bone, wood, and stone.

Games of dexterity included archery, sliding javelins or darts upon the ground, shooting at moving targets such as a netted wheel or ring, ball games in several forms, and racing games including horse racing.[91]

The Hand Game provides a classic example of a game of concealment. Anthropologist Stewart Culin asserts that the game "is played by 81 different tribes from some 28 different linguistic roots."[92] Louis Garcia, honorary historian for the Devils Lake Sioux Tribe, capsulizes the game's essence this way:

The Hand Game is a guessing game played to music in which the hider conceals an object in each hand. Only one of the objects is marked. The guesser points to the hand he or she thinks contains the marked object. If the choice is correct, the guesser wins a counting stick; if not, the guesser loses a counting stick. When one teams wins all the counting sticks, the game is over and that team claims the prize.[93]

In another description of the Hand Game, the editors of Time-Life Books point out: "Wagering can be heavy, and opposing teams constantly attempt to distract each other by beating drums, shaking rattles, and singing taunting songs."[94]

While visiting with the Minnetaree along the Upper Missouri River on November 27, 1833, European explorer Maximilian documented two examples of games of dexterity in his journal:

Young people were playing a game on a long, straight track in the village that is generally called "billiards" by the Whites. Two players run along next to each other and attempt to hit a rolling leather hoop with long spears. . . . Women played a game with a large leather ball. They toss it on the foot and then keep it in the air by kicking it.[95]

Interestingly, whenever a ball was used in an Indian game, it was never touched by the

A lively game of lacrosse among the Sioux. Indian games included ball games like lacrosse, guessing games, archery contests, and races.

hand, since it represented the earth, the sun, or the moon and was considered sacred.

Some Indian games were seasonal. Some adult games were played only during festivals or religious ceremonies, such as archery contests, ball games, sliding arrows or spears on ice or frozen ground, and horse and foot racing. Most children's games helped to prepare the child for adulthood and stressed dexterity, competition, and endurance. Typically, boys played at tracking and concealment with their peers, while girls competed in cooking, sewing, beadworking, and other female activities. Perhaps the most widely known of all Indian

sports is the spirited, physically challenging ball game of lacrosse, so named by French Canadian traders. Played with long-handled nets, under rules similar to those of field hockey, it remains ever popular to this day.

Storytelling

At the end of a long day's work or play, the ancient and honored tradition of storytelling provided the Plains Indians with a fascinating means of relaxation and entertainment. And the enchanting tales of tribal storytellers,

Children of the Sun

Storytelling is intrinsic to the Native American culture. Through the timeless art of storytelling, the Indians of North America have for thousands of years preserved with the spoken word their tribal histories, mythologies, anecdotes, and wisdom. One of the more popular tales narrated in one form or another by virtually all American tribes is the creation story. In American Indian Myths and Legends, *Richard Erdoes and Alfonso Ortiz retell the charming tale of how the Osage "Children of the Sun" came to be.*

"Way beyond the earth, a part of the Osage lived in the sky. They wanted to know where they came from, so they went to the sun. He told them that they were his children. Then they wandered still farther and came to the moon. She told them that she gave birth to them, and that the sun was their father. She said that they must leave the sky and go down to live on earth. They obeyed, but found the earth covered with water. They could not return to their home in the sky, so

they wept and called out, but no answer came from anywhere. They floated about in the air, seeking in every direction for help from some god; but they found none.

The animals were with them, and of these the elk inspired all creatures with confidence because he was the finest and most stately. The Osage appealed to the elk for help, and he dropped into the water and began to sink. Then he called to the winds, and they came from all quarters and blew until the waters went upward in mist.

At first only rocks were exposed, and the people traveled on the rocky places that produced no plants to eat. Then the waters began to go down until the soft earth was exposed. When this happened, the elk in his joy rolled over and over, and all his loose hairs clung to the soil. The hairs grew, and from them sprang beans, corn, potatoes, and wild turnips, and then all the grasses and trees."

—*From Alice Fletcher and Francis LaFléche, who recorded this myth in 1911.*

handed down through the years by word of mouth, furnished each succeeding generation with another window into its past.

Nothing piques the interest of most people as does a tale well told. And surely there are few better ways to learn history than to gather round the campfire and listen to a storyteller spin yarns of yesteryear. Many of their legends were simple animal tales about wildlife on the plains and prairies.

Imagine, for example, a Cheyenne family in their tipi in the early dark of a cold winter night. A Cheyenne elder commences his narration of "The Story of the Earth," which, he says, will explain why some Cheyenne do not eat beaver:

> The earth rests on a large beam or post. Far in the north there is a beaver, as white as snow, who is a great father of all mankind. Some day he will gnaw through the support at the bottom; we shall be helpless, and the earth will fall. This will happen when he becomes angry. The post is already partly eaten through. For this reason one band of Cheyennes never eat beaver, or even touch the skin. If they do touch it, they become sick.

And perhaps he tells another Cheyenne tale to remind them of their brief claim on mortality and the inevitability of lasting "Death":

> When first created, the people gathered to see if they were to live or die. If a stone floated in water, they were to live; if it sank, they were to die; but to a buffalo chip opposite conditions were attached. The stone was thrown in. For a moment it remained at the surface, and all the people rejoiced, thinking to live forever; then it sank. So the chip was thrown in, and for a moment it sank out of sight, and again they rejoiced; but then it rose and drifted away. The short time that the stone floated and the chip sank represents the shortness of man's life before lasting death.[96]

There are many such legends in Indian lore, and for every legend a legion of listeners. Tales are told and retold without end. New tales continue to evolve. And each tale evokes in the mind's ear of every wide-eyed listener unique imaginings of some part of his or her being, or of nature, the world, the universe—the scheme of things entire.

Warriors and Wars

"I would rather die an Indian than live a white man."

—Sitting Bull, Hunkpapa medicine man and paramount chieftain of the Lakota (quoted in Robert M. Utley, *The Lance and the Shield*)

Life on the plains meant two things to male Indians: hunting and warring. Preparations for fulfilling their roles as hunters and warriors began before they were born. Their mothers- or grandmothers-to-be prepared quilled or beaded turtle and sand lizard amulets. Both creatures, hard to kill, symbolized long life. Such charms were intended to transmit like qualities to their owners. At birth, the male child's umbilical cord was cut and inserted into the turtle amulet, packed in herbs or tobacco, to remind the child that life was a gift from its parents. The sand lizard acted as a decoy to lure away the forces of evil.

Parents spent endless hours instructing children in the virtues of spirituality, pride, respect for their elders, as well as others and their property, and conformance to tribal ethics and established rules of etiquette. As often as not, a mother's lullaby contained a lesson in morals or courage. And tribal elders instructed the young in tribal history and loyalty.

A father started training his son somewhere between the ages of four and seven in the use of bow and arrows, and shortly thereafter began teaching the boy the techniques of hunting and trailing. Often the equivalent of an Indian godfather or an older boy would help in a youth's training. By the time a boy reached the age of ten, he was fully involved in learning the basic skills required of Indian manhood.

Making and Handling Weapons

Bows and arrows were the most important implements in the Indians' weapons arsenal. The sustenance and protection of their tribe depended on them. Accordingly, adult males gave high priority to training young males not only to become proficient but to become expert in the handling and making of bows and arrows.

Indian boys learned first to shoot for distance with the bow and arrow, moving on to accuracy training after the required distance was achieved. Buffalo chips often served as targets, initially as stationary marks placed at an established distance. Later, when a boy's aim produced three hits through the center of the chip in five shots, his mentor would roll the chip to provide a more challenging moving target.

Since speed of delivery was of vital importance in hunting and warfare, boys were taught to hold one or more extra arrows in their left hand to speed up their rate of fire. Most boys became incredibly proficient at rapid fire by maturity, as the following description by Thomas E. Mails indicates:

Shooting, handling, and making bows and arrows were among the most vital skills Indians learned as boys and perfected as adults. Here, the Mandan practice archery.

The remarkable thing about a mature Indian and his bow was the rapidity and force with which he could send his arrows. He could seize from five to eight in his left hand, fire the first of them in a high arch, and then discharge the rest so rapidly that the last would be in the air before the first had struck the ground. In the midst of a furious battle he could launch his arrows with such force that each could mortally wound a man at twenty yards.[97]

An Indian youth also learned to make weapons. A good bow took about a month to

make, and making arrows required expert craftsmanship. The various woods used in the making of both often required seasoning and curing for many months. Indian craft experts Marz and Nono Minor explain:

Some of the Plains tribes gathered their wood for bows in the very early spring while the sap was still down. This insured that the wood would season with little danger of shrinkage and splitting. When cut and trimmed, the green bow stave was covered with bear grease and hung high up in the tipi so the smoke of the fire and not the flames could reach it.

When the wood was properly seasoned, it was shaped and rubbed smooth with a piece of sandstone. . . . Bowstrings were made of sinew or vegetable fibers. The string was tied to notches at one end of the bow, and the noosed end was slipped over the notch at the opposite end.

Most bows were straight when unstrung, but some were curved. The curve was shaped by greasing the bow, heating the wood over a fire until hot, and bending and holding the wood in the desired shape with the foot until the wood cooled and the curve took a permanent set. Sinew was then glued to the roughened flat back of the bow. Wood for arrows underwent a similar seasoning and straightening process. According to the Minors:

Usually each man made his own arrows, and they were more intricate to make than the bow. Seldom were two arrows of the same length and each man could recognize his own arrows. Every arrow had an owner mark on it to identify which arrows killed the game. . . . [After seasoning, curing, and straightening] the sticks were drawn through a stone or deer's horn in which holes had been made, as a means of [further] straightening the arrow stick. The sticks were finally twirled between sandstone to polish them and finish off the final shaping.[98]

The diameter of the finished shaft ranged from about .3 to .5 inches; length varied from about 24 to 29 inches. Blackfoot, Sioux, and Cheyenne shafts measured about 25.5 inches long. Arrowheads of flint, bone, shell, wood, or metal were bound to the front end of the shaft and feathers of the eagle or some other bird were glued to the rear end to complete the arrow.

Other weapons used to good advantage by the Plains Indians included knives, clubs, hatchets, lances, and eventually guns. With the exception of the latter, the Indian fashioned them all himself, as always calling on natural resources for materials. And as with bows and arrows he spent countless hours learning to use them with maximum efficiency.

Boys into Men

The Indian boy's path from boyhood to manhood was difficult and demanding. In the horse-dominated life of the plains, it was essential for all tribal members, especially the males, to ride well. Hunting, tracking, and survival skills had to be mastered before a boy reached his teens, at which time his training grew even more intense.

Many Indian sources indicate that most Plains boys became adept at riding without adult supervision by their fifth or sixth year. Nor did girls lag far behind in acquiring riding skills. As noted by author Elaine Andrews:

Both boys and girls became expert riders. Indian horses had no saddles and the bridles were a piece of rope looped around a horse's lower jaw. Children learned to guide their swift ponies by the pressure of their knees and legs, just as the adults did.

Shooting at targets, racing their ponies, watching the men make the hunting gear and weapons were all practice for the time when a boy would join the hunt or a war party.[99]

Fathers and other adult instructors passed along to Indian boys a variety of hunt-

An 1834 painting by George Catlin shows Comanche feats of riding, including sliding to one side of the horse and hanging on by the heels and a loop around the horse's neck, while still shooting arrows.

ing and tracking skills garnered through many years of bountiful application. Writes Indian authority Carl Waldman:

> Many different methods were used, including individual stalking and grabbing with bare hands; communal free-drives or surrounds; pursuing with dogs and horses; or capturing with traps, snares, pits, and poisons. Hunting weapons included spears, clubs, atlatls [dart- or spear-throwing sticks], bows and arrows, slings, [and] bolas [weighted cords for throwing and entangling animals].

Equally important skills for tracking humans and game animals—that is, reading their signs and following them—were also handed down to the future trackers. Waldman adds:

> A tracker relied on changes in the environment, such as broken vegetation, moved stones, foot and animal prints, and droppings, as well as knowledge of the countryside and intuition to follow their enemy or prey.[100]

Perhaps nothing in the Indian boy's training was more vital than learning how to survive alone in the wilderness. As Thomas

This hide painting shows two warriors in battle. Warfare was a major part of life on the plains, and boys learned survival and tracking skills in preparation.

E. Mails writes, with obvious admiration for his subject:

> An Indian youth on the Plains may not have had reading and writing and arithmetic to learn, but he had the alphabet and calculations of the wilderness to conquer, and that alone involved the learning of a thousand signs, any combination of which must be read and acted upon immediately in order that he might triumph and live. . . .
>
> The Indian boy not only saw things non-Indians missed, but he saw them when they were farther away. When he couldn't see them he could put his ear to the ground and find them by their sounds. Beyond that, he could smell as well as the wolf. He was always at attention, looking, calculating, measuring his chances of success. He was honed by his elders until his reactions were sharp and instant. Panic was out. When caught off guard he must automatically spot the enemy, estimate what would happen next, whether he should fight or run, and above all think more of giving warning to others than of saving himself.[101]

Upon his mastery of these basic skills, the aspiring warrior-to-be moved on to a more advanced and dangerous curriculum.

Indian Warfare

Before the horse brought mobility to the Plains Indians, disputes of any consequence between tribes were infrequent and short-lived. Plains tribes lived, hunted, and otherwise functioned most of the time within the limits of a fairly well-defined home country and generally coexisted peacefully with their neighbors. But with the advent of the horse, raiding and warfare became a way of life for Indian males—and for some females. Carl Waldman writes:

> Native Americans fought defensive war to protect families, homes, and lands as well as aggressive war to take spoils and seek revenge. Warfare generally was a man's activity, as when war parties were sent out, but women often fought side by side with men in defensive war.[102]

In offensive war, participation in war or raiding parties was usually voluntary. Any warrior invited to join a party of either kind was free to decline if he felt that bad medicine might be associated with the group or activity. In defensive war, however, men between the fighting ages of fifteen and thirty-five were honor bound to belong to a large war party. Tribal defense was everyone's responsibility.

"To Gain Honor and Glory"

The term *warfare* did not carry the same connotation for Indians—who viewed it almost as a sport—as it did for whites. As Elaine Andrews observes:

> It was not warfare as many people think of it, with large armies marching to meet each other and then doing battle. Plains war was a series of swift raids by one group against another. The basic idea was to gain honor and glory by avenging an attack or better yet, by capturing as many horses as possible. Taking horses was a

major objective of raids, not because a tribe necessarily needed them, but because the possession of horses was a sure sign of success—and prestige.

Despite the "sporting" aspects of such raids they were hardly less deadly than conventional warfare, as Andrews points out:

> Raids of one tribe upon another brought counterattacks for revenge. Some tribes became bitter enemies, seemingly in constant warfare. Territorial disputes were one cause, as a tribe tried to move into another's territory. The Sioux fought the Shoshone, who came onto the Plains from the mountains. Around the Arkansas River in the southern Plains, the southern Cheyenne fought the Comanche and the Kiowa.[103]

In a classic study of Indian warfare, anthropologist Bernard Mishkin, who did fieldwork among the Kiowa in 1935, later wrote:

> In native thought war parties are differentiated at every point according to whether they are for horse raiding or for revenge.

> The size of a raiding party was from 6 to 10 men. Occasionally 1 or 2 men, perhaps brothers, might go off alone to seek their fortune, and again a large body of warriors, 20 to 30 or more, would sometimes go off for horses. The revenge party, on the other hand, was usually larger. A hundred or 200 warriors was the customary size for such a party although some were smaller. These figures, then, corroborate the principle that raiding parties generally issued from the *topotóga*,

[band], that is to say, all the men comprising a war [raiding] party would belong to the same *topotóga*, while the revenge parties because of their size were tribal in character. The duration of a war party varied roughly with its size. The small raiding parties could stay out almost indefinitely and in some cases a few men were known to be gone for a year or two. Revenge parties were compelled to return in short order so that other activities of the tribe, mainly hunting, could go on.

"The return of a successful raiding party, in common with the return of the revenge party," concludes Mishkin, "was met with great rejoicing and was the occasion for celebration."[104]

Perhaps Thomas E. Mails has captured the flavor of Indian warfare during the golden age of the Plains Indians as well as it can be stated:

This was the way of life for the Indian warriors of all the Plains tribes. To them, the swift raids and the miniature wars were part of a very good life in which the

The success of a raiding party was a source of great glory, and the return of the warriors (pictured) was cause for celebration. Raids usually resulted in a revenge attack by the raided group, however.

When whites moved onto the plains in the mid-1800s and established settlements like Fort Union (pictured), clashes between Indians and the U.S. Army ensued.

days were enjoyed, not measured. As they put it, it was "the time when our hearts sang for joy."[105]

War for the Plains

When the Europeans came, killed off the life-sustaining buffalo, and sought to strip the Indians of their lands, a war to the death between red men and whites commenced. The editors of Time-Life Books summarily characterized the passing of the golden age of the Plains Indians this way:

> The war for the Great Plains, one of the epic tragedies of American history, was kindled in the mid-19th century by the intrusion of white migrants on the home-

lands and hunting grounds of the Indians. Within a few decades, the vast open range west of the Mississippi River was riven with thoroughfares for white emigrants. And by 1890, the region's original inhabitants—tribes whose territories stretched from the Canadian wilderness to the deserts of northern Mexico—had suffered total military defeat and a devastating transformation from free hunters and warriors to impoverished wards of the burgeoning nation.[106]

From 1850 to 1865 the U.S. Army engaged in some thirty separate small wars or major disturbances involving the Indians, including the Sioux, Cheyenne, Arapaho, Kiowa, and Comanche. One of the more famous encounters between Indians and

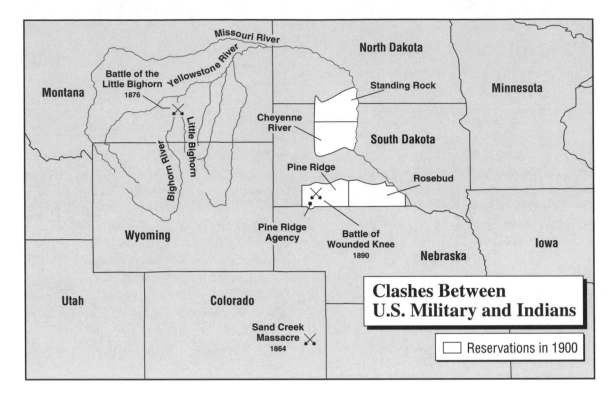

Clashes Between
U.S. Military and Indians

☐ Reservations in 1900

whites—and perhaps the most shameful incidents of white treachery—occurred toward the end of this period in Colorado.

On November 29, 1864, Colonel John M. Chivington led seven hundred Colorado militiamen in a surprise attack against a village of Cheyenne and Arapaho, while their leaders were trying to negotiate a treaty. When three militia officers protested that it was murder to kill unarmed Indians, Chivington roared, "Damn any man who sympathizes with Indians! I have come to kill Indians, and believe it is right and honorable to use any means under God's heaven to kill Indians." [107]

Chivington and his raiders killed two hundred Indians, mostly women and children, during what became known as the Sand Creek Massacre. Historians largely credit this onerous affair as likely the principal cause for escalating hostility of the Plains Indians in the following two decades.

Between 1865 and 1898, the U.S. Army fought 943 actions in twelve separate campaigns against the Indians west of the Mississippi River. Notable among these campaigns were the Sioux and Cheyenne War, 1876–1877, and the Sioux War in South Dakota, 1890–1891. Out of these conflicts the Indians gained one spectacular victory over the white man's army.

On June 25, 1876, beside Montana's Little Bighorn River, approximately two thousand Sioux and Cheyenne warriors, led by Sitting Bull and Crazy Horse, annihilated an entire column of the U.S. Seventh Cavalry, including its commander, Lieutenant Colonel George Armstrong Custer. Afterward, Red Horse, a Sioux council chief, recalled, "The Sioux did not take a single soldier prisoner, but killed all of them; none were alive for even a few minutes." [108] The Sioux and Cheyenne won that battle but lost the campaign when Colonel Nelson A. Miles defeated Crazy Horse at Wolf Mountain, a spur of the Bighorn range, on January 8, 1877.

By 1881 the last of the Plains tribes had been removed from their homelands—the lands of their ancestors—and exiled on government-assigned reservations. Free spirits that had soared like eagles across the plains for centuries were caged forever by the white man. But sporadic Indian resistance continued for nine more years on the plains.

In 1889 Wovoka, a Paiute Indian in Nevada known as Jack Wilson, revived the Indian religion of the Ghost Dance. Wovoka, the Paiute messiah,

The Clash at Wounded Knee

In The American Heritage History of the Indian Wars, *historian Robert M. Utley recounts the clash at Wounded Knee Creek this way:*

"Although the Sioux awoke on December 29 with a sense of fear and distrust, neither they nor the troopers intended to have a fight. There were only 350 Indians, and 230 of these were women and children. Furthermore, the soldiers had been strengthening during the night by the other squadron of the regiment and now counted about 500 men. Colonel James W. Forsyth had taken command. He posted his men on all sides of the Indian camp. From a nearby hill four Hotchkiss cannon pointed at the tepees. Clearly resistance would be suicidal. For his part, Colonel Forsyth planned to disarm the Indians and escort them to the railroad, in Nebraska, to be taken out of the zone of military operations.

But as the soldiers began to search for the Indians' guns powerful emotions built up on both sides. A medicine man pranced about inciting the men to fight—their ghost shirts [ceremonial shirts worn by Ghost Dancers that supposedly would stop bullets] would protect them. The troopers grew more and more nervous. One seized a deaf man to take away his rifle. It went off. The medicine man tossed a handful of dirt in the air. A knot of warriors threw off their blankets and leveled their Winchesters at a rank of cavalrymen. Both sides fired at once, and the fight that neither side intended or expected burst upon them.

The clash at Wounded Knee was a horror of murderous fighting. Soldiers and Indians faced each other at close range and shot, stabbed, and clubbed one another. A bullet shattered Lieutenant John C. Gresham's elbow. Another carried away the top of Captain George C. Wallace's head. A warrior slashed at interpreter Philip Wells with a long knife and left his nose hanging by a shred of skin. Weakly [the ill chief] Big Foot rose from his pallet to watch. A volley killed him and most of the other chiefs behind him. As the two sides separated, the Hotchkiss guns went into action, each belching forth 50 rounds a minute. The exploding shells flattened the Indian camp and filled the air with deadly flying fragments. A participant remembered seeing a shell punch a six-inch hole in a man's stomach. Caught in the fire women and children went down along with the men. In less than an hour most of the fighting had ended. The battlefield was a scene of carnage. Almost two thirds of Big Foot's band had been cut down—at least 150 dead and 50 wounded. The army lost 25 killed and 39 wounded."

fell into a trance and returned to consciousness preaching that by performing a circular dance and adhering to certain principles of virtuous and peaceful living, Indians could restore their lands and recover their own deceased ancestors.[109]

News of the religion spread swiftly throughout the western tribes and led directly to the death of Sitting Bull and the symbolic end of the war for the plains.

End of a Lifeway

Eventually, Lakota from the Sioux reservations at Pine Ridge and Rosebud in South Dakota adopted the Ghost Dance and began dancing and experimenting with their new religion. Whites mistook their dancing for unrest and feared a rebellion.

On November 15, 1890, Daniel F. Royer, the Indian agent at Pine Ridge, wired his Washington superiors: "Indians are dancing in the snow and are wild and crazy. We need protection and we need it now."[110] When U.S. cavalry and infantry reinforcements appeared at Pine Ridge five days later, some three thousand Lakota seeking refuge "camped together in a remote and rugged natural fortress called the Stronghold."[111]

One month later to the day, Sitting Bull, the great Hunkpapa medicine man and paramount chief of the Sioux, was slain while trying to evade capture in a skirmish at the

The Ghost Dance was revived in 1889 among the Paiute and quickly became popular among other tribes, including the Arapaho, shown here performing the dance.

Death of a Dream

After the carnage at Wounded Knee Creek, on December 29, 1890, Oglala holy man Black Elk and some sixty of his followers

Oglala chief Red Cloud (1822–1909) delivered a poignant speech to his followers after the clash at Wounded Knee.

wanted to seek revenge against the White soldiers. But Oglala war leader Red Cloud talked them out of more fighting. In Black Elk Speaks, *Black Elk recalled that Red Cloud said something like this:*

"'Brothers, this is a very hard winter. The women and children are starving and freezing. If this were summer, I would say to keep on fighting to the end. But we cannot do this. We must think of the women and children and that it is very bad for them. So we must make peace, and I will see that nobody is hurt by the soldiers.'"
Commented Black Elk:
"And the people agreed to this, for it was true. . . .
And so it was all over.
I did not know then how much was ended. When I look back now from this high hill of my old age, I can still see the butchered women and children lying heaped and scattered all along the crooked gulch as plain as when I saw them with eyes still young. And I can see that something else died there in the bloody mud and was buried in the blizzard. A people's dream died there. It was a beautiful dream."

Standing Rock Agency and Reservation in North Dakota. On the Cheyenne River Agency and Reservation in South Dakota, Miniconjou chief Big Foot, upon hearing of Sitting's Bull's death, decided to move his band to a more protected area of the Pine Ridge Reservation.

Chief Big Foot—once a Ghost Dance advocate but by then disenchanted with it—sought peace. When intercepted en route by a detachment of the Seventh Cavalry, Big Foot surrendered. The Miniconjou band camped for the night beside Wounded Knee Creek.

On the morning of December 29, 1890, Seventh Cavalry troops, following a night of celebrating Big Foot's capture, entered the Miniconjou camp to disarm the Indians. An altercation arose and a shot rang out. The melee that followed lasted less than an hour, synopsized by historian Alan Axelrod as follows:

Big Foot and 153 other Miniconjous were known to have been killed. So many others staggered, limped, or crawled away that it is impossible to determine just how many finally died. Most likely, 300 of the 350 who had been camped at Wounded Knee Creek lost their lives. The Seventh Cavalry had its casualties, too: 25 killed and 39 wounded.[112]

The distinguished military historians R. Ernest Dupuy and Trevor Dupuy emphati-cally deny that the clash at Wounded Knee was a massacre, as it has come to be known by many. "The 7th Cavalry thus gained revenge for its defeat on the Little Big Horn," they write. "This was the last major Indian conflict."[113]

Controversy continues to haunt the incident at Wounded Knee but one aspect of it remains unassailable. Robert M. Utley writes, "After Wounded Knee, the Sioux resignedly submitted to the reservation system and thus implicitly surrendered the last vestiges of its sovereignty to the invader."[114]

The Caged Eagle

"The nation's hoop is broken and scattered. There is no center any longer, and the sacred tree is dead."

—Black Elk, *Black Elk Speaks*

The tragic affair at Wounded Knee ended a way of life for the Plains Indians and consigned those proud people to the restricted indignities of reservation life. The eagle had been caged.

Indian Reservations

"Reservations were first created by seventeenth century English colonizers and imposed on American Indian nations to remove them from the path of white settlement," writes James Riding In, a Pawnee and assistant professor of justice studies at Arizona State University. Continuing, he states:

> The United States took up this practice, employing military might, fraud, and deception to create hundreds of tribal reserves, established by treaty, executive order, or congressional decree. Despite the reservations' grim origins, Indian people have been able to adapt to reservation environments while preserving many of their traditional values, beliefs, and customs. In fact, many Indians now regard reservations as homelands.[115]

In many respects today's reservations resemble small towns. Self-sustaining and blending into the countryside almost beyond notice, they typically contain an Indian agency or other federal offices, tribal offices, schools, stores, and churches. Until the 1960s, most tribes sustained themselves on the natural resources of their surroundings, engaging in such occupations as ranching, farming, fishing, and logging. Since then, government-funded programs have helped to develop technological skills and business acumen among reservation dwellers, contributing to enhanced tribal economies. Increased tourism and Indian gaming casinos have also added to the prosperity of some tribes.

Notwithstanding some gains in the Indian community, all is far from well on the 278 Indian land areas federally recognized as reservations. These reservations currently comprise less than 2 percent of their original area and house some 950,000 Indians—not quite half of the total Indian population.

Moreover, non-Indians hold title to significant parcels of reservation lands. Also, according to James Riding In, the land owned by Indians

> is usually held "in trust" by the federal government, meaning that this property is exempt from state and county taxes and can be sold only in accordance with federal regulations.

Although both paternalism and anti-Indian racism exist, Indian governments have reinvigorated their reservations by

Reservation Indians collect rations at a government store in this 1882 illustration. Reservations have recently become more economically self-sufficient due to tourism and casinos.

adopting tax codes, establishing profitable enterprises, organizing courts, drafting law-and-order codes, controlling their resources, and demanding a right to worship in customary ways [often forbidden by government edict]. Nonetheless, many small, landless, and isolated native nations have been able to gain few benefits. As a result, economic, health, and social problems still haunt many reservations.

"The challenge facing Indian governments and federal policymakers," Riding In reminds both factions, "continues to be to devise ways

of improving reservation living conditions in ways that support tribal self-government, traditional culture, and religious freedom."[116]

Indian Dilemma

On the reservation, the transition period from 1890 to the present has been arduous and life disrupting for most Indians. Marred by economic deprivation and the policy vacillations of the federal government, Native Americans today still live in a limbo not of their own making. As Philip J. Deloria, acclaimed Lakota author and professor of history at the University of Colorado, apprises:

Indians have fought . . . to maintain Indian identities and social cohesiveness even as they live, work, and play in a society that prides itself on being a huge "melting pot." Americans love to bandy the phrase about, but in practice we have frequently reaffirmed *differences* of race, ethnicity, class, religion, gender, sexuality, and geography that have allowed us to hold meaningful group and personal identities. What too many of us have failed to do, however, is to accept the uncertainty that inevitably accompanies a society cherishing both the idea of shared values and of a diverse multiculturalism. Instead, as American Indian policy demonstrates, Americans have bounced back and forth between unity and diversity, one year trying to force the minorities to assimilate, the next recognizing and embracing the differences.[117]

Song of Little Wolf

Great Powers, hear me,
The people are broken and scattered.
Let the winds bring the few seeds together,
To grow strong again, in a good new place.

—Little Wolf, Cheyenne chief
(quoted in Mari Sandoz,
Cheyenne Autumn)

Caught between a compelling need to preserve ancient heritages and the lure of integrating into a modern global society, today's Indians face a dilemma that neither they nor Washington lawmakers have so far been able to resolve.

New Hope

Meanwhile, life on the reservation goes on. But more now than ever, Indians are demanding a stronger voice in their own affairs. Tribal leaders and Indian politicians and activists are pressing harder and harder to regain treaty rights and lost lands through courts of law and public opinion. And a growing number of native voices seem to be expressing new hope for a conciliation of cultures and a better tomorrow. In the words of Cree-Flathead-Shoshone artist Jaune Quick-to-See Smith:

In my half-century of life, I've witnessed extreme poverty, poor health care, infant mortality levels that are twice the national average, the highest suicide rates in the U.S., and unemployment as high as 80 percent. But today there is a newly awakened pride in tribal life and a new vitality in our communities. I see energy, determination, conviction, and vision among our tribal people.[118]

The "newly awakened pride" and "new vitality" of Native Americans resound in the words of Gros Ventre activist George Horse Capture: *"We are here now, have been here for thousands of years, and we will always be here. We have fooled them all!"*[119]

Notes

Introduction: The Plains and the People

1. Quoted in Richard Erdoes and Alfonso Ortiz, eds., *American Indian Myths and Legends*. New York: Pantheon Books, 1984, p. 95.
2. Quoted in Elaine Andrews, *Indians of the Plains: The First Americans*. New York: Facts On File, 1991, p. 8.
3. Vine Deloria Jr., "The So-Called Bering Strait Theory," in David Hurst Thomas et al., *The Native Americans: An Illustrated History*. Atlanta: Turner Publishing, 1993, p. 28.
4. N. Scott Momaday, "My American Indian Ancestors," in Thomas et al., *The Native Americans*, p. 26.
5. Thomas E. Mails, *The Mystic Warriors of the Plains*. New York: Barnes & Noble, 1991, p. 2.
6. Richard White, "The Shedding of Blood," in Clyde A. Milner II et al., eds., *The Oxford History of the American West*. New York: Oxford University Press, 1994, pp. 277, 281.
7. Quoted in Judith Nies, *Native American History: A Chronology of a Culture's Vast Achievements and Their Links to World Events*. New York: Ballantine Books, 1996, p. 273.
8. Quoted in Robert M. Utley and Wilcomb E. Washburn, *The American Heritage History of the Indian Wars*. New York: Barnes & Noble, 1977, p. 266.

Chapter 1: Daily Life on the Plains: Dwellings

9. Black Elk, as told through John G. Neihardt, *Black Elk Speaks*. 1932. Lincoln: University of Nebraska Press, 1988, p. 9.

10. Terry P. Wilson, "Osage," in Frederick E. Hoxie, ed., *Encyclopedia of North American Indians*. Boston: Houghton Mifflin, 1996, p. 449.
11. James Welch with Paul Stekler, *Killing Custer: The Battle of the Little Bighorn and the Fate of the Plains Indians*. New York: W. W. Norton, 1994, p. 49.
12. Reginald and Gladys Laubin, *The Indian Tipi: Its History, Construction, and Use*. Norman: University of Oklahoma Press, 1957, p. 15.
13. Frederick E. Hoxie, "Tipi," in *Encyclopedia of North American Indians*, p. 629.
14. T. R. Fehrenbach, *Comanches: The Destruction of a People*. New York: Da Capo Press, 1994, p. 108.
15. Maximilian zu Wied, *People of the First Man: Life Among the Plains Indians in Their Final Days of Glory: The Firsthand Account of Prince Maximilian's Expedition up the Missouri River, 1833–34*. New York: E. P. Dutton, 1976, pp. 186, 230.
16. Andrews, *Indians of the Plains*, p. 25.
17. Bruce Grant, ed., *Concise Encyclopedia of the American Indian*. Rev. ed. New York: Wings Books, 1994, pp. 66–67.
18. George Catlin, *North American Indians*. New York: Penguin Books, 1996, pp. 74–75.
19. Mails, *The Mystic Warriors of the Plains*, p. 21.
20. John Redtail Freesoul, *Breath of the Invisible: The Way of the Pipe*. Wheaton, IL: The Theosophical Publishing House, 1986, p. 48.

Chapter 2: Daily Life on the Plains: Families and Functions

21. Maximilian, *People of the First Man*, p. 127.

22. The Editors of Time-Life Books, *Tribes of the Southern Plains*. The American Indian series. Alexandria, VA: Time-Life Books, 1995, p. 31.
23. Mark St. Pierre and Tilda Long Soldier, *Walking in the Sacred Manner: Healers, Dreamers, and Pipe Carriers—Medicine Women of the Plains Indians*. New York: Simon and Schuster, 1995, p. 48.
24. George Bird Grinnell, *By Cheyenne Campfires*. Lincoln: University of Nebraska Press, 1971, p. 9.
25. Marilyn G. Bentz, "Child Rearing," in Hoxie, ed., *Encyclopedia of North American Indians*, p. 118.
26. David Hurst Thomas, "Life of the Plains and Woodlands," in Thomas et al., *The Native Americans*, pp. 94–95.
27. Mails, *The Mystic Warriors of the Plains*, p. 581.
28. Catlin, *North American Indians*, p. 10.
29. The Editors of Time-Life Books, *Tribes of the Southern Plains*, pp. 27–28.
30. Josephine Paterek, *Encyclopedia of American Indian Costume*. New York and London: W. W. Norton, 1994, p. 84.
31. Grinnell, *By Cheyenne Campfires*, p. xxiii.
32. St. Pierre and Long Soldier, *Walking in the Sacred Manner*, p. 18.
33. Quoted in Mails, *The Mystic Warriors of the Plains*, p. 35.

Chapter 3: Character and Customs

34. George E. Tinker, "Religion," in Hoxie, ed., *Encyclopedia of North American Indians*, p. 539.
35. Quoted in St. Pierre and Long Soldier, *Walking in the Sacred Manner*, p. 14.
36. Marz and Nono Minor, *The American Indian Craft Book*. Lincoln: University of Nebraska Press, 1978, pp. 168–69.
37. Maximilian, *People of the First Man*, pp. 243–44.
38. Bentz, "Child Rearing," in Hoxie, ed., *Encyclopedia of North American Indians*, p. 117.
39. Marz and Nono Minor, *The American Indian Craft Book*, pp. 165–66.
40. St. Pierre and Long Soldier, *Walking in the Sacred Manner*, p. 79.
41. Jay Miller, "Families," in Hoxie, ed., *Encyclopedia of North American Indians*, p. 196.
42. Norman Bancroft-Hunt, *The Indians of the Great Plains*. Norman: University of Oklahoma Press, 1992, p. 45.
43. Donald J. Berthrong, "Elders," in Hoxie, ed., *Encyclopedia of North American Indians*, p. 179.
44. Bancroft-Hunt, *The Indians of the Great Plains*, p. 45.
45. Berthrong, "Elders," in Hoxie, ed., *Encyclopedia of North American Indians*, p. 179.
46. Maximilian, *People of the First Man*, p. 244.
47. Catlin, *North American Indians*, pp. 93–94.
48. Henry F. Dobyns, "Diseases," in Hoxie, ed., *Encyclopedia of North American Indians*, p. 164.
49. Quoted in Mails, *The Mystic Warriors of the Plains*, p. 74.

Chapter 4: Tribal Government

50. Quoted in Robert M. Utley, *The Lance and the Shield: The Life and Times of Sitting Bull*. New York: Henry Holt, 1993, p. 9.
51. Mails, *The Mystic Warriors of the Plains*, pp. 77, 86.
52. Welch, *Killing Custer*, p. 123.
53. Fehrenbach, *Comanches*, p. 44.
54. Utley, *The Lance and the Shield*, p. 9.
55. The Editors of Time-Life Books, *Tribes of the Southern Plains*, p. 54.
56. Utley and Washburn, *The American Heritage History of the Indian Wars*, p. 194.

57. Quoted in Mails, *The Mystic Warriors of the Plains*, p. 82.
58. David Humphreys Miller, *Custer's Fall: The Native American Side of the Story*. New York: Penguin Books, 1992, p. 258.
59. Andrews, *Indians of the Plains*, p. 62.
60. Grant, *Concise Encyclopedia of the American Indian*, p. 112.
61. Quoted in Mails, *The Mystic Warriors of the Plains*, p. 56.
62. Andrews, *Indians of the Plains*, p. 64.

Chapter 5: Religion and Medicine

63. St. Pierre and Long Soldier, *Walking in the Sacred Manner*, p. 48.
64. Freesoul, *Breath of the Invisible*, pp. 8–9.
65. Arlene Hirschfelder and Paulette Molin, *The Encyclopedia of Native American Religions*. New York: MJF Books, 1992, p. 307.
66. Mails, *The Mystic Warriors of the Plains*, p. 132.
67. Quoted in Mails, *The Mystic Warriors of the Plains*, p. 107.
68. Carl Waldman, *Word Dance: The Language of Native American Culture*. New York: Facts On File, 1994, p. 136.
69. Quoted in Bancroft-Hunt, *The Indians of the Great Plains*, p. 98.
70. Marz and Nono Minor, *The American Indian Craft Book*, p. 134.
71. Jennie R. Joe, "Health and Healing," in Hoxie, ed., *Encyclopedia of North American Indians*, p. 239.
72. Hirschfelder and Molin, *The Encyclopedia of Native American Religions*, p. 67.
73. Mails, *The Mystic Warriors of the Plains*, p. 117.
74. Mails, *The Mystic Warriors of the Plains*, p. 110.
75. Howard L. Harrod, "Death," in Hoxie, ed., *Encyclopedia of North American Indians*, p. 156.
76. Grant, *Concise Encyclopedia of the American Indian*, p. 61.
77. Harrod, "Death," in Hoxie, ed., *Encyclopedia of North American Indians*, p. 156.
78. Quoted in Mails, *The Mystic Warriors of the Plains*, p. 176.

Chapter 6: Arts, Crafts, Games, and Storytelling

79. Phoebe Farris-Dufrene, "Arts, Visual (to 1960)," in Hoxie, ed., *Encyclopedia of North American Indians*, pp. 45, 46.
80. Mails, *The Mystic Warriors of the Plains*, p. 244.
81. Grant, *Concise Encyclopedia of the American Indian*, p. 233.
82. Waldman, *Word Dance*, p. 166.
83. Paterek, *Encyclopedia of American Indian Costume*, p. 85.
84. Farris-Dufrene, "Arts, Visual (to 1960)," in Hoxie, ed., *Encyclopedia of North American Indians*, p. 50.
85. Waldman, *Word Dance*, p. 166.
86. Grant, *Concise Encyclopedia of the American Indian*, p. 234.
87. John Stoutenburgh Jr., *Dictionary of the American Indian*. New York: Wings Books, 1990, p. 343.
88. Paterek, *Encyclopedia of American Indian Costume*, p. 87.
89. Mails, *The Mystic Warriors of the Plains*, p. 245.
90. Marz and Nono Minor, *The American Indian Craft Book*, p. 165.
91. Marz and Nono Minor, *The American Indian Craft Book*, p. 311.
92. Quoted in Louis Garcia, "Hand Game," in Hoxie, ed., *Encyclopedia of North American Indians*, p. 229.
93. Garcia, "Hand Game," in Hoxie, ed., *Encyclopedia of North American Indians*, p. 229.
94. The Editors of Time-Life Books, *Tribes of the Southern Plains*, p. 175.
95. Maximilian, *People of the First Man*, p. 183.

96. Quoted in Terri Hardin, ed., *Legends & Lore of the American Indians*. New York: Barnes & Noble, 1993, pp. 126–27.

Chapter 7: Warriors and Wars

97. Mails, *The Mystic Warriors of the Plains*, p. 401.
98. Marz and Nono Minor, *The American Indian Craft Book*, pp. 285–86.
99. Andrews, *Indians of the Plains*, p. 39.
100. Waldman, *Word Dance*, pp. 104, 240.
101. Mails, *The Mystic Warriors of the Plains*, pp. 521, 523.
102. Waldman, *Word Dance*, p. 254.
103. Andrews, *Indians of the Plains*, pp. 39, 40.
104. Bernard Mishkin, *Rank and Warfare Among the Plains Indians*. Lincoln: University of Nebraska Press, 1992, pp. 28, 31.
105. Mails, *The Mystic Warriors of the Plains*, p. 578.
106. The Editors of Time-Life Books, *War for the Plains*. The American Indian series. Alexandria, VA: Time-Life Books, 1994, p. 7.
107. Quoted in Alan Axelrod, *Chronicle of the Indian Wars: From Colonial Times to Wounded Knee*. New York: Prentice Hall General Reference, 1993, p. 196.
108. Quoted in Dee Brown, *Bury My Heart at Wounded Knee: An Indian History of the American West*. New York: Henry Holt, 1991, p. 296.
109. Frederick E. Hoxie, "Ghost Dance," in Hoxie, ed., *Encyclopedia of North American Indians*, p. 223.
110. Quoted in Utley and Washburn, *The American Heritage History of the Indian Wars*, p. 335.
111. Paul M. Robertson, "Wounded Knee Massacre," in Hoxie, ed., *Encyclopedia of North American Indians*, p. 695.
112. Axelrod, *Chronicle of the Indian Wars*, p. 255.
113. R. Ernest Dupuy and Trevor N. Dupuy, *The Encyclopedia of Military History*. New York: Harper & Row, 1977, p. 907.
114. Robert M. Utley, *The Indian Frontier of the American West 1846–1890*. Albuquerque: University of New Mexico Press, 1984, p. 261.

Afterword: The Caged Eagle

115. James Riding In, "Reservations," in Hoxie, ed., *Encyclopedia of North American Indians*, p. 546.
116. Riding In, "Reservations," in Hoxie, ed., *Encyclopedia of North American Indians*, pp. 548–49.
117. Philip J. Deloria, "What the Indians Can Teach Us," in Thomas et al., *The Native Americans*, p. 462.
118. Quoted in Deloria, "What the Indians Can Teach Us," in Thomas et al., *The Native Americans*, p. 464.
119. Quoted in Nies, *Native American History*, p. 307.

Glossary

atlatl: A stick, usually about sixteen to twenty inches long, used for throwing darts or spears.

axis mundi: World axis; central axis to the universe.

bola: A weighted cord for throwing and entangling animals.

Ghost Dance: An Indian religion preaching that by performing a circular dance and adhering to certain principles of virtuous and peaceful living, Indians could restore their lands and recover their own deceased ancestors.

ghost shirt: A ceremonial shirt worn by Ghost Dancers that supposedly would stop bullets.

mandala: A Hindu or Buddhist graphic symbol of the universe; specifically, a circle enclosing a square with a deity on each side.

modus operandi: Method of procedure.

parfleche: A rawhide soaked in lye to remove the hair, then dried; a bag made from this material.

pemmican: A concentrated food consisting of lean, dried, and pounded meat mixed with melted fat.

pictograph: A picture or sign representing a word or idea as opposed to a sound.

piquet: A pointed or sharpened stake, post, or pale; variant of picket.

topotóga: Kiowan for band; an extended family group.

Chronology of Events

1700

Sioux move from the woodlands to Minnesota, and then to the Black Hills—forcing the Crow and Cheyenne on just ahead of them.

1775

Most of the shifting of tribes on the Great Plains ends; permanent domains are established.

Late 1700s

Traders arrive on the plains bringing beads and other trade items.

Early 1800s

A loose alliance among the Sioux, the Arapaho, and the Cheyenne dominates the northern plains.

1831–1837

American artist George Catlin travels extensively among the native peoples of North America, notably including the Lakota, Mandan, Pawnee, and Comanche tribes of the plains.

1833–1834

Prince Maximilian zu Wied, the German explorer and naturalist, and Karl Bodmer, his Swiss-born artist companion, follow the broad Missouri River for some five thousand miles, during a year-long sojourn with the Plains Indians.

1850–1865

U.S. Army engages in some thirty separate small wars or major disturbances involving the Indians.

1864

November 29: Sand Creek Massacre; 700 Colorado militiamen kill 200 peaceful Cheyenne and Arapaho.

1865–1898

U.S. Army fights 943 actions in twelve separate campaigns against the Indians west of the Mississippi River.

1876–1877

The Sioux and Cheyenne War.

1876

June 25: The Battle of the Little Bighorn.

1877

January 8: Colonel Nelson A. Miles defeats Crazy Horse at Wolf Mountain in the Bighorn range.

1881

The last of the Plains tribes now removed from their homelands.

1889

The Ghost Dance religion revived in Nevada.

1890

December 29: Clash at Wounded Knee Creek, South Dakota, between Miniconjou Sioux and U.S. Seventh Cavalry; symbolic end of the war for the plains.

1891

January 15: Four thousand Sioux surrender to Brigadier General Nelson A. Miles near White Clay Valley, north of the Pine Ridge Agency.

For Further Reading

Evan S. Connell, *Son of Morning Star*. New York: Promontory Press, 1984. Author Connell tells the story of the Plains Indians' last great victory against the white man.

Jerome A. Greene, ed., *Lakota and Cheyenne: Indian Views of the Great Sioux War, 1876–1877*. Norman: University of Oklahoma Press, 1994. Indian descriptions of the Plains people's struggle to protect their homelands, families, and tribal cultures.

William T. Hagan, *United States–Comanche Relations: The Reservation Years*. Norman: University of Oklahoma Press, 1990. The author tells how the proud Comanche were transformed into apathetic wards of the U.S. government.

Jon E. Lewis, *The Mammoth Book of the West: The Making of the American West*. New York: Carroll and Graf, 1996. The story of what life was really like on the western frontier.

Thomas E. Mails, *The People Called Apache*. New York: BDD Illustrated Books, 1993. A classic work on nearly every aspect of the Apache culture.

Charles M. Robinson III, *A Good Year to Die: The Story of the Great Sioux War*. New York: Random House, 1995. The author recounts events during the crucial year of 1876, when hostilities between the U.S. government and the Indian Nations peaked.

Mari Sandoz, *Crazy Horse: The Strange Man of the Oglalas*. Lincoln: University of Nebraska Press, 1992. Sandoz portrays the troubled life of the great Oglala chieftain.

John Edward Weems, *Death Song: The Last of the Indian Wars*. New York: Indian Head Books, 1991. Weems focuses on the lives and actions of several leaders among both the Indians and the whites.

Works Consulted

Elaine Andrews, *Indians of the Plains: The First Americans*. New York: Facts On File, 1991. Andrews recounts the lifestyles of eleven of the better-known Indian tribes of the Great Plains.

Alan Axelrod, *Chronicle of the Indian Wars: From Colonial Times to Wounded Knee*. New York: Prentice-Hall General Reference, 1993. A sweeping narrative of the Indian Wars from the time the Europeans first landed in America until their final confrontation with the Indians at Wounded Knee.

Norman Bancroft-Hunt, *The Indians of the Great Plains*. Norman: University of Oklahoma Press, 1992. A superbly written and illustrated validation of the Plains Indians and their way of life amid the rare beauty of the Great Plains.

Black Elk, as told through John G. Neihardt, *Black Elk Speaks*. 1932. Lincoln: University of Nebraska Press, 1988. Black Elk recounts the story of the Oglala Sioux, from the Custer battle to the Wounded Knee massacre.

Winfred Blevins, *Dictionary of the American West*. New York: Facts On File, 1993. This remarkable dictionary recaptures the unique language of the American West and provides enjoyable, informative reading from cover to cover.

Dee Brown, *Bury My Heart at Wounded Knee: An Indian History of the American West*. New York: Henry Holt, 1991. Brown allows the great chiefs and warriors of the plains to tell in their own words of the battles, massacres, and broken treaties.

George Catlin, *North American Indians*. New York: Penguin Books, 1996. A one-volume edition of Catlin's journals, with more than fifty reproductions of his incomparable paintings of North American Indian life.

R. Ernest Dupuy and Trevor N. Dupuy, *The Encyclopedia of Military History*. New York: Harper & Row, 1977. A monumental work on warfare by two noted historians; includes a keen analysis of the Indian Wars.

The Editors of Time-Life Books, *Tribes of the Southern Plains*. The American Indian series. Alexandria, VA: Time-Life Books, 1995. An illustrated study of the earliest tribes on the southern plains.

———, *War for the Plains*. The American Indian series. Alexandria, VA: Time-Life Books, 1994. An illustrated account of the struggle for the expanding frontier.

Richard Erdoes and Alfonso Ortiz, eds., *American Indian Myths and Legends*. New York: Pantheon Books, 1984. One hundred and sixty-six legends of the native people of North America.

T. R. Fehrenbach, *Comanches: The Destruction of a People*. New York: Da Capo

Press, 1994. Fehrenbach tells the story of the powerful Comanche who rode into modern history in a headlong collision with Western civilization.

————, *The Indian Frontier of the American West 1846–1890*. Albuquerque: University of New Mexico Press, 1984. Dramatic events of the final half-century of conflict between Indians and whites in the American West presented as a history of two peoples seemingly destined never to understand each other.

Russell Freedman, *The Life and Death of Crazy Horse*. New York: Holiday House, 1996. The captivating story of the Oglala Sioux chieftain known as "Our Strange One" to his people.

John Redtail Freesoul, *Breath of the Invisible: The Way of the Pipe*. Wheaton, IL: The Theosophical Publishing House, 1986. Traces the dramatic revival of the ceremonial pipe of the Plains Indians as a tool for seeking self-knowledge and harmony with the Creator, neighbors, and the environment.

Bruce Grant, ed., *Concise Encyclopedia of the American Indian*. Rev. ed. New York: Wings Books, 1994. More than eight hundred entries covering all aspects of Indian history and culture; well organized, easy to use, and highly readable.

George Bird Grinnell, *By Cheyenne Campfires*. Lincoln: University of Nebraska Press, 1971. Cheyenne folktales about their heroes, their wars, and their relationships with supernatural powers.

————, *The Fighting Cheyennes*. North Dighton, MA: JG Press, 1995. An essential study of the Cheyenne and their place among the Indian tribes of the western plains; includes many firsthand accounts by participants on both sides of the Indian Wars.

Terri Hardin, ed., *Legends & Lore of the American Indians*. New York: Barnes & Noble, 1993. An extraordinary collection of Native American legend and lore drawn from a wealth of material gathered together by both storytellers and scholars.

Arlene Hirschfelder and Paulette Molin, *The Encyclopedia of Native American Religions*. New York: MJF Books, 1992. An in-depth reference for the general reader that examines Native American beliefs and spiritual traditions in more than 1,200 entries.

Frederick E. Hoxie, ed., *Encyclopedia of North American Indians*. Boston: Houghton Mifflin, 1996. Written by more than 260 contemporary authorities on Indian life past and present, this ambitious volume represents a valuable sourcebook on the varieties of Native American experience.

Alvin M. Josephy Jr., *500 Nations: An Illustrated History of North American Indians*. New York: Alfred A. Knopf, 1994. A splendidly illustrated account of American history from the Native American viewpoint.

Howard R. Lamar, ed., *The Reader's Encyclopedia of the American West*. New York:

Harper & Row, 1977. A broad but detailed view of western history; contains more than 2,400 entries examining "the people, places, institutions, and ideas that collectively define the American frontier experience."

Reginald and Gladys Laubin, *The Indian Tipi: Its History, Construction, and Use*. Norman: University of Oklahoma Press, 1957. The complete story of this fascinating Indian tent—its history and development, the different types and locations, furnishings, and etiquette.

Thomas E. Mails, *The Mystic Warriors of the Plains*. New York: Barnes & Noble, 1991. A classic work defining the lifestyles of the Plains Indians when they were still relatively untouched by the white man's progress.

David Humphreys Miller, *Custer's Fall: The Native American Side of the Story*. New York: Penguin Books, 1992. The story of Custer's Last Stand from an Indian perspective.

Clyde A. Milner II et al., eds., *The Oxford History of the American West*. New York: Oxford University Press, 1994. A comprehensive compendium that combines the work of twenty-eight historians to render full treatment to the rich complexities of this vast region.

Marz and Nono Minor, *The American Indian Craft Book*. Lincoln: University of Nebraska Press, 1978. A thorough guide to the crafts of the North American Indian tribes in the seven basic cultural areas; interesting and informative.

Bernard Mishkin, *Rank and Warfare Among the Plains Indians*. Lincoln: University of Nebraska Press, 1992. A classic study examining the Indians' economic motivations in waging war and their changing relations with other peoples.

Judith Nies, *Native American History: A Chronology of a Culture's Vast Achievements and Their Links to World Events*. New York: Ballantine Books, 1996. An enlightening timeline spanning three hundred centuries, juxtaposing Native American achievements with those of their European counterparts.

Josephine Paterek, *Encyclopedia of American Indian Costume*. New York and London: W. W. Norton, 1994. "A beautifully produced and illustrated reference that offers complete descriptions and cultural contexts of the dress and ornamentation of the North American Indian tribes." —*Book News*

Mari Sandoz, *Cheyenne Autumn*. Lincoln: University of Nebraska Press, 1992. The tale of the Cheyenne Indians who attempt to return to their homeland in the Yellowstone country against the will and military might of a major emerging nation.

John Stoutenburgh Jr., *Dictionary of the American Indian*. New York: Wings Books, 1990. An A-to-Z guide to Indian history, legend, and lore.

Mark St. Pierre and Tilda Long Soldier, *Walking in the Sacred Manner: Healers, Dreamers, and Pipe Carriers—Medicine Women of the Plains Indians*. New York: Simon and Schuster, 1995. An exploration of the myths and cultures of the Plains Indians.

John Upton Terrell, *American Indian Almanac*. New York: Barnes & Noble, 1994. Terrell traces Native Americans from their mystery-shrouded beginnings until March 25, 1916, when "the last wild Indian in America" died.

David Hurst Thomas et al., *The Native Americans: An Illustrated History*. Atlanta: Turner Publishing, 1993. This companion to the landmark TBS television series spans a thousand generations of original Americans, from the Ice Age to the present.

Robert M. Utley, *The Indian Frontier of the American West 1846–1890*. Albuquerque: University of New Mexico Press, 1984. An engrossing account of the dramatic events of the final half-century of conflict between Indians and whites.

———, *The Lance and the Shield: The Life and Times of Sitting Bull*. New York: Henry Holt, 1993. A vivid historical biography that corrects many misconceptions about Sitting Bull—one of the nation's greatest Native Americans.

Robert M. Utley and Wilcomb E. Washburn, *The American Heritage History of the Indian Wars*. New York: Barnes & Noble, 1977. An impressive volume that covers four hundred years of bloody conflict between the Indians and their white conquerors.

Carl Waldman, *Word Dance: The Language of Native American Culture*. New York: Facts On File, 1994. "A fine review of word origins in the Native American languages." —*Bookwatch*

Peter Watts, *A Dictionary of the Old West 1850–1900*. New York: Wings Books, 1977. A totally enjoyable reference source of the colorful western idiom.

James Welch with Paul Stekler, *Killing Custer: The Battle of the Little Bighorn and the Fate of the Plains Indians*. New York: W. W. Norton, 1994. The authors tell the story of the Battle of the Little Bighorn from an Indian perspective.

Prince Maximilian zu Wied, *People of the First Man: Life Among the Plains Indians in Their Final Days of Glory: The First-hand Account of Prince Maximilian's Expedition up the Missouri River, 1833–34*. New York: E. P. Dutton, 1976. Beautiful art, intriguing ethnology, and gripping true adventure blended to tell the story of the proud Plains Indians.

Index

Picture Credits

Cover photo: Corbis-Bettmann
Archive Photos, 16, 32, 68
Archive Photos/American Stock, 35
The Bettmann Archive, 13, 18, 50, 71, 78
Corbis-Bettmann, 38, 47, 52, 70, 75, 85
Courtesy, Colorado Historical Society (F36,899), 45
Library of Congress, 12, 22, 28, 29
National Archives, 25, 37, 84
National Museum of American Art, Washington DC/Art Resource, NY, 10, 19, 21, 77

Peter Newark's American Pictures, 67
Peter Newark's Western Americana, 20, 44, 46, 64, 80
The Thomas Gilcrease Institute of American History and Art, 62, 81
UPI/Bettmann, 63
UPI/ Corbis-Bettmann, 27, 31, 54
Werner Forman Archive/Art Resource, NY, 48, 55, 57, 61, 66

About the Author

Earle Rice Jr. attended San Jose City College and Foothill College on the San Francisco peninsula, after serving nine years with the U.S. Marine Corps.

He has authored twenty-two books for young adults, including fast-action fiction and adaptations of *Dracula, All Quiet on the Western Front*, and *The Grapes of Wrath*. Mr. Rice has written numerous books for Lucent, including *The Cuban Revolution, The O.J. Simpson Trial, The Final Solution*, and seven books in the popular Great Battles series. He has also written articles and short stories, and has previously worked for several years as a technical writer.

Mr. Rice is a former senior design engineer in the aerospace industry who now devotes full time to his writing. He lives in Julian, California, with his wife, daughter, two granddaughters, four cats, and a dog.